BRANDYWINE
AMERICAN HISTORY WORKBOOK

Volume I

Brandywine Press • Maplecrest, New York

Contents

INSTRUCTIONS
for Students

The exercises in this workbook are an informal way to help you do well on quizzes and hour exams that are based on your American history survey text. Your teacher may ask you to tear off some pages along the perforations and hand them in or to turn in the entire workbook at the end of the semester. Answers to some questions may be found on the website: **www.brandywine-sources.com** But it will not help you if you simply copy them into the workbook. What they can do is show you what you don't know, so you must try your hand first at the questions without benefit of the answers. Once you check your answers and fill out the parts of the workbook not on the website, you will be ready to take exams in your course. Your instructor may even include on the class tests a few of the multiple choice or other questions from this workbook.

The exercises are no substitute for a careful reading of the text by a student who thinks back at what is in print. The purpose is to sharpen that reading. The workbook concentrates on factual detail, but that is to encourage you to respect detail as a beginning toward your understanding of the larger forces of American history. If the workbook helps you to go beyond the detail, to a critical understanding of the nation's history, it will have done its task.

The longer instructions before each part of the first chapter will not be repeated in further chapters. Here are some suggestions for the use of the major exercises:

For each workbook chapter, the sections TERMS and VOCABULARY contain words and phrases that have a significant connection to the textbook chapter. Some of these are important for what they called up in the minds of Americans at some point in the nation's past. An instance is "natural rights." To an educated American of the late eighteenth century or the early nineteenth, the term would have been of enormous philosophical and moral value. Other phrases refer to more tangible things: institutions, events, laws, or whatever. Among these will be phrases that in themselves refer to no particular era, no special part of the world. "Navigable river," for example, could relate to any river of its kind in any country in any century. You will learn, however, that in the early nineteenth century rivers that could be navigated were essential to binding together the sprawling stretches of the young United States.

The section entitled PHOTOGRAPHS rests on the assumption that a view of someone or something, either caught directly in a photo or drawn or painted and then reproduced photographically, invites imaginative responses on the part of a viewer. What of the photograph of an African, imprisoned in a net, and awaiting sale as a slave? What thoughts might have possessed the victim? You will have no direct knowledge. Yet some attempt at wondering should sharpen your awareness that history has been lived, suffered, and occasionally triumphed over by such unnamed people as the photograph catches.

For the exercises labeled INDIVIDUALS, and for the TRUE FALSE and the MULTIPLE CHOICE sections, the basic requirements are self-evident. The TRUE FALSE questions that give specific numbers of people or things are intended not to encourage memorization but to make more specific and concrete your sense of a particular time in American history and to test your judgment. Note that for the MULTIPLE CHOICE questions you are asked to circle the letter before each statement that is correct and that often there is more than one correct answer.

The final section of each workbook chapter, offering topics for essays or oral reports, is the most ambitious. In few if any instances can you write a satisfactory essay on the basis of information drawn solely from the text. It is supposed that you will know before beginning a topic, or learn in the course of responding to it, how to use a library or one of the internet Web search engines. Some of the documents on **www.brandywinesources.com** should be useful. For an entire semester a student, at the direction of the instructor, may have time for only one topic drawn from one workbook chapter, or the project may be reserved for students aiming at extra credit. Or your instructor may use topics for oral discussions or brief essays in which you simply suggest how to go about a more extended response. The compilers of the workbook tried not to patronize you by assuming you are capable of nothing other than memorization or by failing to provide challenging questions in which you can exhibit to your instructor, your classmates, and yourself that you are up to the game.

Origins and Beginnings

1

A. TERMS—For each of these, indicate the meaning of the word or phrase.
(Your instructor may request that you tear out along the perforations some or all of the pages in this workbook and hand them in.)

origin stories _____
_____
_____

swidden agriculture _____
_____
_____

language families _____
_____
_____

selective breeding _____
_____
_____

social hierarchies _____
_____
_____

Protestant Reformation _____
_____
_____

wattle-and-daub _____
_____
_____

domestication _____
_____
_____

nomadic _____
_____
_____

B. PHOTOGRAPHS

1. Put yourself in the position of the man at left. What do you suppose to be his thoughts about his home, the people who captured and sold him, the traders who purchased or will soon purchase him, and what he expects of his future life? Use your imagination, but also look up at your library, on Brandywine's internet site, and on other reliable sites some data on how the slave trade operated.

_____

_____

_____

_____

_____

_____

_____

_____

_____

_____

_____

_____

_____

_____

_____

_____

_____

_____

_____

_____

_____

_____

_____

_____

2. Develop a brief hypothetical lineage from this man to a present-day American, including places, occupations, marriages, and the way the imagined family responded to historical events. (Note: you do not have to assume that this figure's descendants would be classified as African American. He could have been sold in Virginia at a time when European and African servants worked alongside each other in the tobacco fields, and intermarried. Some of his descendants may have been classified as white and others as black, some of the latter being free and others enslaved.)

_____

_____

_____

3. Write a speech from this African Benin chief to the Portuguese in the background. What would he have said about his people, his authority, his expectations for trade? What would the Portuguese have said, and how would the chief respond to it?

_____

_____

_____

_____

_____

_____

_____

_____

_____

_____

_____

4. Assume that Venus, at the moment of her birth, had a divine understanding that in the distant future Botticelli's painting of the event would be adopted as a trademark by Adobe Corporation. What would Venus have thought of her image's being used to sell computer software? As an immortal goddess created by the culture of ancient Greece, would she have been pleased at the Renaissance?

_____

_____

_____

_____

_____

_____

_____

_____

_____

_____

_____

_____

_____

_____

_____

_____

_____

_____

_____

_____

_____

_____

_____

_____

_____

_____

_____

_____

_____

_____

_____

_____

_____

_____

_____

_____

C. VOCABULARY—For each of these, indicate the meaning of the word as used in the chapter.

anthropologist _____

_____

archaeologist _____

_____

circumnavigation _____

_____

daimyo _____

_____

dynasty _____

_____

glaciers _____

_____

_____

indigenous _____

_____

_____

linguistics _____

_____

_____

paleontologist _____

_____

_____

Renaissance _____

_____

_____

sectarian _____

_____

_____

D. INDIVIDUALS—Identify each of these people.

Olaudah Equiano _____

_____

Mato Tope (Four Bears) _____

_____

Zheng He _____

_____

Marco Polo _____

_____

Sikandar Lodhi _____

_____

Ashikaga Yoshimasa _____

_____

Prince Henry the Navigator _____

_____

Vasco da Gama _____

_____

Ferdinand of Aragon _____

_____

Isabella of Castile _____

_____

Martin Luther _____

_____

John Calvin _____

_____

Leonardo daVinci _____

_____

Michelangelo Buonarrotti _____

_____

Johannes Gutenberg _____

_____

Nicolaus Copernicus _____

_____

Galileo Galilei _____

_____

E. MATCHING Match each origin story to the people who created it. Not every answer will be found directly in the textbook though clues may be found there; an enterprising search of the library or the internet will find them all.

___ Doondari   a) Indian
___ P'an Ku   b) Tewa
___ Prajapati   c) Fulani
___ turtle   d) cosmologists
___ Dokibatl   e) Chinese
___ Clovis people   f) Huron
___ Blue Corn Woman   g) Nisqually
___ Big Bang   h) paleontologists

SELF-TEST QUESTIONS
(matching, true/false, multiple choice)
The answers will be found on the Brandywine website:
www.brandywinesources.com

Match each crop to the region where it was domesticated.

Crop		Region
___millet	___rice	a) South America
___wheat	___squash	b) South Asia
___beans	___potatoes	c) Europe and Asia
___rye	___oats	d) North and Central America
___corn	___sorghum	e) Africa
___barley		

Match each of these North American regions to the description of its environment.

___Northeast	a) wet forests, cedars
___Southeast	b) prairie, grasslands
___Pacific Northwest	c) cactus, mesas, deep river canyons, arid landscapes
___Southwest	d) hardwood forests, hills, bogs, brush
___Plains	e) piney woods, river valleys, lowland vegetation

Circle the items traded across the African continent through Timbuktu.

gold, silver, ivory, groundhogs, nuts, pumpkins, camels, noodles, grain, amber, ebony,

coal, slaves, turpentine, millet, potatoes, dates

F. TRUE FALSE—circle one.

1. T F The world's greatest navy in the fifteenth century belonged to China.
2. T F Ferdinand Magellan captained the first European ship known to have circumnavigated the globe.
3. T F The Ming dynasty in China exercised power through a collection of strong regional dynasties.
4. T F Africa and Asia shared extensive trade routes by ships crossing the Indian Ocean.
5. T F The Qu'ran provided for the freeing of slaves.
6. T F Hunting cultures in North America treated their quarry with respect.
7. T F Muskogean peoples of the southeastern United States were descended from the Mississippi Moundbuilder culture.
8. T F Native Americans throughout the continent lived in nomadic hunting cultures.
9. T F Christopher Columbus was the first to discover America.
10. T F Many signers of the Declaration of Independence owned slaves.
11. T F Scientists constantly find it necessary to revise origin stories.
12. T F Islamic caliphates provided a safe haven for Jewish communities during the medieval period.
13. T F Spanish conquest forced settlements in Mesa Verde and Chaco Canyon to be abandoned.
14. T F Swidden agriculture fertilized fields to produce several crops every year.
15. T F Portuguese missionaries brought the first iron-smelting technology to Africa.
16. T F Human beings entered America after the last Ice Age came to an end.
17. T F On the islands of Madeira and São Tomé, Portugal established sugarcane plantations with slave labor from Africa.
18. T F Christopher Columbus sought a land where liberty and democracy could flourish.
19. T F The Ottoman Turks' capture of Constantinople interrupted European trade with Asia.

G. MULTIPLE CHOICE—circle one or more correct answers.

1. Tenochtitlán was the capital of
   a) Spain.   b) Kongo.   c) Aztec Mexico.   d) the Holy Roman Empire.   e) Brazil.

2. Olmec and Maya cultures arose in
   a) the Andes Mountains.
   b) Central Asia.
   c) East Africa.
   d) Central America and Mexico.
   e) Japan.

3. Cahokia was the main center of
   a) the transatlantic slave trade.   d) the Inca empire.
   b) Islamic pilgrimage.   e) British colonial manufacturing.
   c) Mississippi Moundbuilding culture.

4. Inuit lived in the _____ environment.
   a) tropical   b) arctic   c) temperate rain forest   d) arid mountainous   e) dry plains

5. Shoshone and Paiute lived in the
   a) Great Basin.   d) Mississippi bayous.
   b) Appalachian Mountains.   e) Amazon jungle.
   c) Great Lakes area.

6. Genetic variation and differences in language suggest that people have lived in the Americas for about
   a) ten million years.   d) several thousand years.
   b) one million years.   e) eight hundred years.
   c) a thousand years.

7. Lummi, Nootka, and Haida cultures obtained their primary food from
   a) irrigated crops.   d) ocean fishing and whaling.
   b) buffalo hunting.   e) cactus and jicama roots.
   c) swidden agriculture.

8. The Anasazi people in the Four Corners region were ancestors of the
   a) *Californios*.   d) Dene (Navajo).
   b) Hopi, Tewa, and other Pueblo Indians.   e) Diablos Tejanos.
   c) Germanic tribes of Europe.

9. The Big Bang theory is an origin story that
   a) tells us creation grew out of the barrel of a gun.
   b) denies the existence of God.
   c) was invented by deaf scientists.
   d) suggests the universe we know began with an explosive burst of energy.
   e) describes life on earth as emerging from a volcano.

10. Prince Henry of Portugal was named The Navigator because
   a) he sailed a ship around the world in 1415.
   b) it was an honored name among Portuguese street gangs.
   c) he encouraged advances in science and technology for building and sailing ships.
   d) he led a great naval victory against the Ottoman Turkish fleet.
   e) he wrote primitive software that allowed ships to sail directly to their destination.

11. When Portuguese ships reached the Cape of Good Hope, the crews knew that
   a) their souls would be guaranteed a place in heaven.
   b) they could sail around Africa from the Atlantic Ocean to the Indian Ocean.
   c) the southern end of Africa would be a good climate to grow sugarcane.
   d) no enemy would be able to follow their route.
   e) Portugal would not have to fight any more wars in their lifetime.

12. The prosperity of Italian city-states like Venice, Genoa, and Florence was based on
   a) subsidies from the Roman Catholic Church.
   b) conquest of Swiss and German provinces to the north.
   c) trade in silks and spices from the east and south.
   d) tax exemptions ordered by the Holy Roman Emperor.
   e) tourist industries offering rest and entertainment for bands of mercenaries.

13. The fifteenth-century German craftsman Johannes Gutenberg invented the
    a) process for smelting steel used by Krupp Industries.
    b) compass used by sailors to tell which way was north.
    c) glaze used to make Dresden china plates.
    d) astrolabe that allowed sailors to identify the latitude at which their ship had arrived.
    e) printing press that allowed mass production of books and newspapers.

14. Martin Luther nailed his Ninety-five Theses on the door of the Roman Catholic cathedral in Wittenberg, Germany, to
    a) kick off his campaign to be chosen as the next Pope.
    b) announce the formation of a church that would allow priests to marry.
    c) call for an increase in tithes and offerings to finish building St. Peter's Basilica.
    d) discuss what he saw as corruption among officials and practices of the church.
    e) ask that all good Germans try to come to church more often.

15. Astronomy in the Americas before Europeans arrived was
    a) based on elaborate techniques and complex math.
    b) unknown, because telescopes had not been introduced.
    c) suppressed by primitive religious beliefs about the stars and sun.
    d) mostly a matter of telling stories based on the shapes of constellations.
    e) difficult to study without the aid of electric lights.

H. ESSAY QUESTIONS OR ORAL REPORTS

FOR MANY QUESTIONS IN THIS WORKBOOK THE PRIMARY SOURCES ON THE INTERNET SITE **www.brandywinesources.com** WILL BE HELPFUL.

You will not find the answers to all of these questions in your textbook. Particularly for oral reports, you will have to look up more specialized sources. For most essay questions, moreover, there is no "correct" answer. This is an opportunity to present your own opinion, with one important consideration: Cite a documented source for anything you quote or assert unless the fact or interpretation is generally known. You should give your own opinion such weight as information and analysis support. These instructions will not be repeated for similar questions pertaining to other chapters in this workbook.

1. Select between two and five origin stories. Compare features that all of your selected stories have in common. Write about some major differences between stories. (For example, how much alike are the Old Testament book of Genesis, the cosmological theory known as the "Big Bang," and the Chinese narrative of P'an Ku, and how do they differ from one another? Or how do Native American origin stories compare with such tales in Asia, Europe, and Africa? What themes in the Doondari poem reflect the account of creation in the Christian Bible, leading from the Hebrew Old Testament to the New Testament account of the birth and resurrection of Jesus?) In what circumstances did each of these stories arise?

2. How did Portuguese exploration, conquest, and trade lay the foundations for slavery as it developed in North America? What use of slaves did Portugal make before developing trade with Africa? How was Portugal introduced to the slave trade within Africa? What crops did Portugal develop using slave labor? Where and when? What nations or their colonies provided markets for the Portuguese to sell slaves? What nations began to take the slave trade away from the Portuguese?

3. How did Roman Catholicism contribute to the settlement of North America? Look at how competition among churches, and among nations committed to an official church, shaped European attitudes toward America. Do not forget that French settlement in Canada, as well as that of the Spanish in the Southwest, established a strong Roman Catholic presence—how did this influence British government policy, and the policies of various British colonies?

4. Summarize the history of corn (maize) from the wild teosinte plant to the food supply we know today. Include cultivation by early Maya and Aztec cultures, the spread of corn through the Americas, the adoption and use by Europeans, and the modern development of hybrids.

5. Read a copy of the Iroquois Constitution, formally known as the *The Great Binding Law, Gayanashagowa*, presented by Dekanawidah to the Confederate Lords of the Five Nations. It is readily available on the internet at www.brandywinesources.com. Compare it with one or more of these: the Magna Carta of England, the Constitution of the United States, and the Charter of the United Nations. For each document you examine, consider the economic life and culture of the people who produced it.

Contact 2

A. TERMS

biological strategies _____
_____
_____

chain of command _____
_____
_____

co-invaders _____
_____
_____

genetic mutation _____
_____
_____

just war _____
_____
_____

mourning wars _____
_____
_____

sickle-cell trait _____
_____
_____

virgin soil epidemics _____
_____
_____

B. PHOTOGRAPHS

Suppose that the Spanish had not drained the lake after conquering the Aztec. Study a map of modern day Mexico City, and read about its industry, neighborhood, and population. Then describe how the city might have developed around the lake. Where would people live? Where would industry be? Would the waters be a beautiful natural resource? How would you plan the growth of the city if you had the authority to do so?

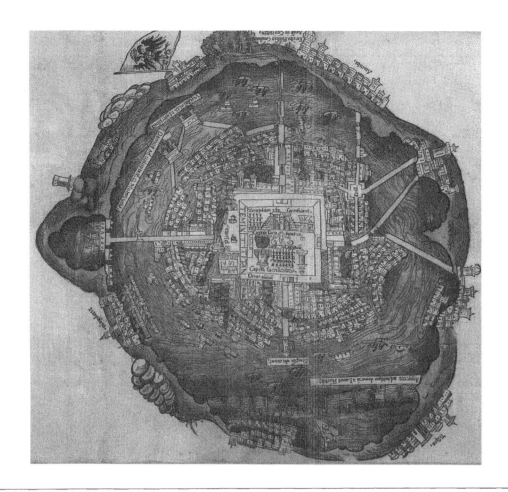

_____
_____
_____
_____
_____
_____
_____
_____
_____
_____
_____
_____

C. VOCABULARY

antibodies _____
_____

assimilation _____
_____

bubonic plague _____
_____

encomienda _____
_____

galleons _____
_____

mestizos _____
_____

métis _____
_____

pathogen _____
_____

pellagra _____
_____

presidio _____

pueblo _____

Reconquista _____

repartimiento _____

scurvy _____

viceroyalty _____

privateers _____

D. INDIVIDUALS

Moctezuma _____

Hernando Cortés _____

Doña Marina (La Malinche) _____

Francisco Pizarro _____

Vasco Núñez de Balboa _____

Bartolomé de las Casas _____

Atahuallpa _____
_____
_____

Pánfilo de Nárvaez _____
_____
_____

Álvar Núñez Cabeza de Vaca _____
_____
_____

Charles I (of Spain) _____
_____
_____

Francisco Coronado _____
_____
_____

Hernando de Soto _____
_____
_____

Juan de Oñate _____
_____
_____

Jacques Cartier _____
_____
_____

Donnacona _____
_____
_____

Samuel de Champlain _____
_____
_____

E. MATCHING Match each individual name with a territory invaded or visited by an expedition that person led.

____Hernando Cortés   a) Peru
____Christopher Columbus   b) New Mexico
____Francisco Pizarro   c) Mexico
____Juan Ponce de Léon   d) Quebec
____Vasco Núñez de Balboa   e) Hispaniola
____Lucas Vazquez de Ayllon   f) Florida
____Francisco Coronado   g) South Carolina
____Hernando de Soto   h) Panama
____Juan de Oñate   i) Alabama
____Jacques Cartier and Samuel de Champlain   j) Kansas

F. TRUE FALSE—circle one.

1. T F One horse could be traded for a hundred Indian slaves in early Spanish settlements.
2. T F Reports of human sacrifice by Aztec priests were exaggerated to justify the Spanish conquest.
3. T F Sugar, tobacco, and rice required intensive labor, which led to dependence on slaves.
4. T F Many city-states outside the Aztec capital barely noticed the Spanish conquest for many years.
5. T F The Council of the Indies was formed by several European nations to coordinate colonial policy.
6. T F Silver mines in northern Mexico and Bolivia helped to fund additional Spanish conquest.
7. T F St. Augustine, Florida, is the oldest continuously occupied European city in the present United States.
8. T F Privateers were state-sponsored pirates unleashed on the shipping of enemy nations.
9. T F Spanish colonial policy was to exterminate Indians and replace them with Spanish men and women.
10. T F Small communities of detribalized Indians were attached to Spanish outposts.
11. T F French settlement in America relied on forced labor from Indians.
12. T F French and British exploration in America was a century behind the Spanish ventures.
13. T F Beaver fur was fashionable because Europe had a plentiful supply of the animals.
14. T F It was Iroquois custom either to kill prisoners swiftly or to return them to the village they came from.
15. T F Factional disputes between Christian converts and other Indians undercut important kinship relations.
16. T F Leaving a few pigs on a Caribbean island provided a labor-free source of meat for passing ships.
17. T F In three well-supplied sieges, Spanish armies failed to conquer the Inca city of Machu Picchu.

G. MULTIPLE CHOICE—circle one or more correct answers.

1. The Black Death, identified most likely as bubonic plague, or some other form of plague
   a) spread from central Asia to Europe along newly established trade routes.
   b) led to higher wages, lower rents, and improved social status for women.
   c) had been cultivated by Chinese scholars for germ warfare against the Mongols.
   d) was successfully treated by Swedish doctors with homeopathic remedies.
   e) was transmitted from the Black Sea around western Europe, and back through Russia.

2. Christóbal Colón is the Spanish form of the name known in other languages as
   a) Cristy Innards.
   b) Christoforo Colombo.
   c) Kris Kringle.
   d) Christopher Columbus.
   e) Crystal Corona.

3. The Taino and Arawak people living on Caribbean islands when Columbus brought Spanish colonists
   a) lived in teepees and attacked the Spanish, riding horses bareback in tight circular formations.
   b) wore jewelry made of gold, which they valued only for its ornamental appearance.
   c) captured and beheaded the Spanish, making slaves of whomever they allowed to live.
   d) rapidly embraced Christianity, volunteering for baptism and forming new religious orders.
   e) were soon eliminated by torture, massacre, rape, enslavement, and disease.

4. The Mayan civilization in the area around the Yucatán peninsula
   a) was destroyed at the peak of its power and culture by the Spanish conquest.
   b) had once possessed a culture far advanced in astronomy and architecture.
   c) never developed centralized administration like that of the Aztec empire.
   d) had broken down politically and presented little effective resistance to the Spanish.
   e) was ruled by an aristocratic priesthood that lived off the labor of the people.

5. Co-invaders brought to the western hemisphere from Europe included
   a) bison and moose.
   b) cattle and horses.
   c) sheep and pigs.
   d) water buffalo and ducks.
   e) groundhogs and mink.

6. Plants were also brought from Europe as co-invaders, including
   a) thistles and dandelions.
   b) clover and nightshade.
   c) trout lily and bunch grasses.
   d) oranges and peaches.
   e) sagebrush and piñon pine.

7. Spanish settlements in the Rio Grande Valley that Coronado explored
   a) were begun in 1598 by Juan de Oñate.
   b) treated residents of pueblos with humanity and respect.
   c) resulted in thousands of conversions to Roman Catholicism.
   d) protected the native population from epidemic diseases.
   e) were interrupted for over ten years by a revolt beginning in 1680.

8. Spanish settlements making use of Indian labor
   a) adapted traditional communal labor duties to obtain free work on farms and ranches of colonists.
   b) effectively prevented physical abuse and murder of workers.
   c) bound workers to silver mines by keeping them constantly in debt.
   d) relied on a free market to obtain workers and set wage levels.
   e) was based on stolen wealth and unpaid labor and established little in the form of solid industries.

9. Military conquest and enslavement of Indians by Spain
   a) was used only for a limited time to establish a foothold in new territory.
   b) produced a theological debate between Juan Gines de Sepulveda and Bartolomé de las Casas.
   c) was stepped up on order from King Charles V.
   d) provided material for the English to create a Black Legend of Spanish brutality.
   e) resulted in the genocide of all Indians in Spanish colonies.

H. ESSAY QUESTIONS OR ORAL REPORTS

1. Considering the political, social, and economic conditions of the lands through which the Black Death spread, give your analysis of the most likely cause.

2. Examine exactly what Christopher Columbus accomplished. What did he set out to do? Were his estimates of world geography accurate? Where did he think he had sailed? On his last voyage, what coast did he believe he was exploring? How did he relate to the populations in possession of the lands he reached? For what purpose? How was he remembered over the next three hundred years? Since most of these questions remain controversial, be especially careful to document the sources of your information; if you find conflicting accounts, document them all, identify which ones you believe are most accurate, and state why.

3. Write a strategy for defeating Hernando Cortés' invasion of the Aztec empire. You can decide whether to assign the strategy to an Aztec leader or a tributary chief who was pleased at the weakening of Aztec rule by the invasion but did not want to see the Spanish become the new ruling power. Account for weapons, terrain, tactics, Spanish use of horses and steel swords, religious beliefs on both sides, reasons many tributary states allied with the Spanish, and the rapid spread of smallpox and other diseases.

4. Examine critically the Black Legend of Spanish brutality. What atrocities really were committed under Spanish rule that are well documented and credible? Who were they committed against, and why? How do these compare with atrocities committed by Spain's enemies? By

previous Native American cultures? What acts and customs under Spanish rule provided for humanity that was lacking elsewhere at the time? Why was Sepulveda, who argued for "just war" against the Indians, considered a leading European humanist?

5. Why did France seek colonies in the Americas? How did the fur trade change the balance of power among different Native American communities between 1580 and 1760? Consider relations among tribes, access to fur-bearing animals, and what activities and traditions for hunting and trapping were replaced among American Indian peoples who took up the fur trade. How did availability of European goods change traditional occupations of Native American life?

The English Colonies

3

A. TERMS

headrights _____
_____
_____

antinomianism _____
_____
_____

Levelers _____
_____
_____

Diggers _____
_____
_____

piedmont _____
_____
_____

right of succession _____
_____
_____

indentured servants _____
_____
_____

House of Burgesses _____
_____
_____

established religion _____
_____
_____

town meeting _____
_____
_____

praying towns _____

_____

_____

Half-Way Covenant _____

_____

_____

B. VOCABULARY

passenger pigeons _____

_____

foraging _____

_____

pasturage _____

_____

potash _____

_____

enclosures _____

_____

tidewater _____

_____

proprietors _____

_____

gentry _____

_____

vestry _____

_____

predestination _____

_____

Separatists _____

_____

_____

conversion _____

_____

salvation _____

_____

covenants _____

_____

dissenters _____

_____

toleration _____

_____

heresy _____

_____

sacrilege _____

_____

patroons _____

_____

thou, thy, thine, and thee as usages in place of "you" _____

_____

mercantilism _____

_____

C. INDIVIDUALS

Queen Elizabeth I _____

_____

King Henry VIII _____

_____

Sir Francis Drake _____

_____

King James I _____

_____

John Cabot _____

_____

Captain John Smith _____

_____

Powhattan _____

_____

Pocahontas _____

_____

Opechancanough _____

_____

John Rolfe _____

_____

George Calvert, Lord Baltimore _____

_____

Sir William Berkeley _____

_____

Nathaniel Bacon _____

_____

Massasoit _____

_____

John Winthrop _____

_____

Thomas Hooker _____

_____

_____

Increase Mather _____
_____
_____

Cotton Mather _____
_____
_____

Roger Williams _____
_____
_____

Anne Hutchinson _____
_____
_____

George Fox _____
_____
_____

John Eliot _____
_____
_____

King Charles I _____
_____
_____

Oliver Cromwell _____
_____
_____

Anne Bradstreet _____
_____
_____

Edward Taylor _____
_____
_____

Metacom _____
_____
_____

Captain Benjamin Church _____
_____
_____

Mary Rowlandson _____
_____
_____

Henry Hudson _____

_____

Peter Stuyvesant _____

_____

King Charles II _____

_____

James, Duke of York (King James II) _____

_____

Sir George Carteret _____

_____

William Penn _____

_____

Sir Edmund Andros _____

_____

William of Orange _____

_____

Jacob Leisler _____

_____

Tituba _____

_____

William Phips _____

_____

William Stoughton _____

_____

Sarah Good _____

_____

28

NAME _____ DATE _____

George Burroughs _____
_____
_____

Ann Putnam _____
_____
_____

D. MATCHING Match these Native American peoples with the approximate territory in which they lived.

___Pawtuxet   a) New York colony
___Narragansett   b) Massachusetts
___Niantic   c) Massachusetts and Connecticut
___Pequot   d) Charles River Valley, Massachusetts
___Wampanoag   e) Rhode Island
___Mohawk   f) Cape Cod, Massachusetts

Match each name at left with the office the individual held at right.

___Elizabeth I   a) Governor of the Dominion of New England
___James VI   b) Archbishop of Canterbury
___Opechancanough   c) Chief of the Wampanoag
___George Calvert   d) Governor of New Netherland
___William Berkeley   e) Proprietor of Pennsylvania
___John Winthrop   f) Lord Protector
___Oliver Cromwell   g) Queen of England
___William Laud   h) King of Scotland
___Metacom   i) Chief of the Powhattan Confederacy
___Peter Stuyvesant   j) Governor of Massachusetts
___William Penn   k) Governor of Virginia
___Sir Edmund Andros l) title of Lord Baltimore

E. TRUE FALSE—circle one.
1. T F Half of the early immigrants to New England came from the region of East Anglia in Britain.
2. T F The Mayflower Compact was the first measure to promote freedom of religion in America.
3. T F Literacy rates in early New England were extremely low; only the wealthiest could read and write.
4. T F Massachusetts hanged several Quakers and whipped many others.
5. T F Trading with Indians took priority over converting them to the Christian faith.
6. T F Deep respect for Indian graves helped the Pilgrims cultivate friendly relations on Cape Cod.
7. T F English settlers sought to multiply the desire of the Indians for new commodities, hoping that this would encourage them to adopt European ways.
8. T F Prisoners captured during or after Metacom's War were sold as slaves to the West Indies.
9. T F Dutch houses in New Netherland were flimsier and more poorly constructed than homes in other colonies.
10. T F A Dutch Reformed minister complained that Jews, atheists, Papists, Mennonites, Lutherans, and Puritans were living in New Netherland.
11. T F Territory where Delaware is located today was settled by Swedes.
12. T F Conestoga wagons were invented by English colonists, who based the design on a farm cart used in Yorkshire.
13. T F Deer became nearly extinct in Massachusetts by 1694.

14. T F After 1672, wild turkeys were easily found and commonly hunted in New England.
15. T F The first ships to Jamestown carried skilled workmen and laborers to carve out a new settlement.
16. T F The government of colonial Virginia highly valued literacy and education.
17. T F Two thirds of the passengers on the *Mayflower* were known as Strangers.
18. T F Wages and prices were regulated by law in Plymouth colony.
19. T F King Charles I granted a charter to Massachusetts Bay Company to reward his friends with land grants.
20. T F Massachusetts, Plymouth, and Connecticut encouraged unmarried people to live with a family.
21. T F Rhode Island was a leading member of the United Colonies of New England.
22. T F Boston in 1700 was a tiny port, smaller than dozens of shipping centers in England and the Caribbean.

F. MULTIPLE CHOICE—circle one or more correct answers.

1. The Glorious Revolution of 1688 in England
   a) established the kingdom of God on earth according to Calvinist precepts.
   b) installed the first republican government in the history of England.
   c) deposed King James II in favor of William of Orange and his wife Mary.
   d) overthrew Oliver Cromwell and legalized dancing around the Maypole.
   e) was motivated by Protestants who did not want a Catholic heir to succeed James as king.

2. Witchcraft during the 1600s in England and North America was
   a) a crime that could be tried in court and punished by law.
   b) a craft possessed by old women and a few men, which has since been lost.
   c) generally understood to be the result of a contract between individuals and Satan.
   d) not well defined, but at times of fear and hysteria, many innocent people were accused.
   e) a common theme for public holidays such as Halloween.

3. When the Virginia colony was first settled at Jamestown,
   a) there was a good harvest the first year, celebrated by a huge feast.
   b) the majority of colonists were unsuited to hard physical labor in an undeveloped land.
   c) Powhattan could easily have wiped out the colonists in the first few years.
   d) Captain John Smith demanded that all decisions be made by majority vote.
   e) searching for gold and jewels was a common practice.

4. Among the fur-bearing animals hunted in New England were
   a) long-horned cattle and bobcats.
   b) otter, muskrat, and mink.
   c) jaguars and ocelots.
   d) weasels, groundhogs, and seals.
   e) beaver, moose, and lynx.

5. The Spanish Armada was
   a) the company that financed Christopher Columbus's second and third voyages to America.
   b) the army that defeated the last Moorish kingdom in Spain and expelled all the Jews.
   c) a fleet prepared by King Philip II of Spain to invade Protestant England.
   d) destroyed by rough seas and by English ships led by Sir Francis Drake and Sir Walter Raleigh.
   e) the beginning of a sixteen-year war in which England took control of Atlantic shipping from Spain.

6. A typical dwelling in the early Chesapeake Bay colonies
   a) lay directly on earth with no wood floors.
   b) contained well-stuffed feather beds with embroidered sheets and patchwork quilts.
   c) was inhabited by people eating from common dishes like European peasants.
   d) had stone piers sunk in the earth so that the supports would not rot.
   e) featured bedrooms opening from a two-story gallery of crude plaster walls.

7. Dutch merchants in the 1600s
   a) were active in developing the slave trade from Africa to America.
   b) lost their American colonies by refusing to hire Hendrick Hudson, who then sailed for England.
   c) financed a mutiny which set back the Hudson's Bay Company by fifty years.
   d) routinely captured Spanish treasure ships.
   e) conducted much of their trade through the Dutch West India Company.

8. The witchcraft trials in Salem, Massachusetts, in 1692
   a) launched the religious revival known as the Great Awakening.
   b) saved Massachusetts colony from a plot to establish Satanic worship as the state religion.
   c) resulted in the executions of twenty people.
   d) relied on sloppy standards of evidence and testimony of spectral apparitions.
   e) were repudiated in 1711 when all convictions were reversed and indemnities paid to survivors.

9. In the colonial south after 1680, plantations
   a) were seized and divided among the servants who had done the primary field work.
   b) could not obtain enough indentured servants and relied increasingly on slaves from Africa.
   c) added rice as a staple cash crop in South Carolina.
   d) turned to cultivation of cotton as a fast way to increase profits.
   e) benefited from the genetic protection some Africans had against malaria.

10. In matters of faith and religion, most New England colonies
   a) guaranteed freedom of conscience and worship to all people.
   b) condemned all churches except the Puritan church, taxing or persecuting dissenters.
   c) tolerated the Roman Catholic Church as more purified than the Church of England.
   d) practiced democracy among those who had a conversion experience and adhered to a covenant.
   e) were especially harsh toward Quakers, who were executed, whipped, or banished.

G. ESSAY QUESTIONS OR ORAL REPORTS

1. Review the types of servitude that developed in different British colonies during the 1600s. What did the words "servant" and "master" mean during this period? Compare the use of labor in the Chesapeake Bay region, put to producing a cash crop, with the role of servants in the Calvinist societies of New England. Also examine practices in the Dutch colony of New Netherland and the development of the Charles Town settlement in South Carolina from the slave labor economy of Barbados. What sort of labor relations in the South were the first Africans woven into after 1619? How did the conditions of servitude among the earlier generation of blacks differ from the slavery of the 1700s?

2. In the early seventeenth century, compare the immigrants to the New England colonies with the settlers in Virginia and Maryland. In each case, what parts of England did the settlers come from? Were any from outside England? For each region examine the occupations and work skills among immigrants to these sections and how prosperous they were. What was the ratio of men to women to children? Had the settlers immigrated voluntarily?

3. Where did monarchs in Europe get the idea that they could give tracts of land in America to their own subjects? Did this grow out of a practice already common in European history? What were the attitudes of conquering settlers toward the people already living in the lands they occupied? By what negotiations did settlers claim title to lands originally inhabited by native peoples? Did the English settlers differ from the Spanish in their way of acquiring title to those lands?

4. Was Nathaniel Bacon a torchbearer of the revolution as one historian once wrote, or did he lead "an army of racists" as Stephen Saunders Webb suggests in *The End of American Independence*? Could both statements be true? Could both be false? What was the significance of Bacon's Rebellion to understanding how colonial Virginia shaped the ideology of the nation we know today? Who fought under Bacon, who opposed him, and why?

5. How did the theology of the Pilgrim and Puritan colonies shape their civil government, economic development, and relations with neighboring peoples?

6. Look up several different accounts of individuals from a European culture who became members of Native American communities, by choice or capture, adoption or assimilation. What made the adopted culture more attractive than the one they had grown up in? Why did some return to their original community and some remain in their new community? Can you find and provide evidence for the same motivations among Native Americans who became part of European colonial communities? Or were the motives and pressures in that case totally different?

Growing British, Becoming American

4

A. TERMS

Inner Light _____

_____

_____

evangelical revival _____

_____

_____

Original Sin _____

_____

_____

Deism _____

_____

_____

Great Awakening _____

_____

_____

Toleration Acts _____

_____

_____

Middle Passage _____

_____

_____

slave codes _____

_____

_____

redemption contracts _____

_____

_____

sumptuary laws _____

_____

Edict of Nantes _____

_____

common law _____

_____

justice of the peace _____

_____

Enlightenment _____

_____

Franklin stove _____

_____

land speculation _____

_____

B. PHOTOGRAPHS

1. Write a paragraph describing the mansion in the background, from the viewpoint of someone inhabiting the quarters in the foreground.

_____
_____
_____
_____
_____
_____
_____
_____
_____
_____
_____
_____
_____
_____
_____
_____
_____
_____
_____
_____
_____
_____

2. Write a paragraph describing the architecture of the slave quarters, and the people who lived there, from the viewpoint of someone living in the mansion.

_____
_____
_____
_____
_____
_____
_____
_____
_____
_____
_____

_____
_____
_____
_____
_____
_____
_____
_____
_____
_____
_____
_____
_____
_____
_____
_____
_____
_____
_____
_____
_____
_____

3. This mansion has an exterior similar to that of many houses built today, and to the exterior of older dwellings that are still in daily use. Find some sources on the architecture and daily life of the eighteenth century. Then write about ways in which the interior of the house differed drastically from the interiors of recent homes. Two areas to include are bathrooms and kitchens. Look for others as well.

_____
_____
_____
_____
_____
_____
_____
_____
_____
_____
_____
_____
_____
_____
_____
_____
_____
_____
_____
_____
_____
_____
_____
_____
_____
_____
_____

C. VOCABULARY

tsetse fly _____
_____

pruning _____
_____

Huguenots _____
_____

libel _____
_____

gentility _____

_____

nobility _____

_____

gentry _____

_____

clientele _____

_____

artisan _____

_____

freeholders _____

_____

aristocrat _____

_____

revivalism _____

_____

sanctification _____

_____

redemption (two meanings) _____

_____

inoculation _____

_____

D. INDIVIDUALS

Benjamin Lay _____

_____

John Woolman _____

_____

_____

James Oglethorpe _____
_____

John Peter Zenger _____
_____

William Byrd II _____
_____

Benjamin Franklin _____
_____

Paul Revere _____
_____

Devereaux Jarratt _____
_____

George Washington _____
_____

Hannah Barnard _____
_____

George Whitefield _____
_____

Jonathan Edwards _____
_____

John Wesley _____
_____

Zabdiel Boylston _____
_____

John Locke _____
_____

Thomas Jefferson _____

_____

_____

Captain George Chicken _____

_____

_____

Robert Dinwiddie _____

_____

_____

Tanaghrisson _____

_____

_____

Major General Edward Braddock _____

_____

_____

Neolin _____

_____

_____

E. MATCHING Match each college in the middle column with the colony it was located in, at the line in center left, and its religious affiliation at the time of founding, at the line in center right.

a) Connecticut	__ __Harvard	A) none
b) New Jersey	__ __William and Mary	B) Puritan
c) Massachusetts	__ __Yale	C) Congregationalist
d) Virginia	__ __Princeton	D) Church of England
e) New York	__ __King's (Columbia)	E) Presbyterian
f) Rhode Island	__ __College of Philadelphia	F) Baptist
g) Pennsylvania	__ __Brown	G) Unitarian
h) New Hampshire	__ __Dartmouth	H) Methodist

Indicate which statements are consistent with the teachings of the Enlightenment **[E]**, the Great Awakening **[A]**, or both **[B]**:

[ ] confidence in human intelligence and benevolence
[ ] sinners' need for redemption
[ ] faith and virtue in pursuit of a calling
[ ] reliance on Scriptural revelation
[ ] Original Sin inherited from the disobedience of Adam and Eve
[ ] a life of moral and charitable conduct
[ ] toleration of a variety of religious expression
[ ] direct personal experience of conversion
[ ] popular participation and initiative
[ ] rigorous intellectual inquiry

F. TRUE FALSE—circle one.
1. T F Europeans engaged in the slave trade had easy access to all areas of Africa.
2. T F British authorities practiced germ warfare against Indians by giving them blankets infected with smallpox.
3. T F People who were captured and sold into slavery were seldom tempted to commit suicide.
4. T F The transatlantic slave market altered the nature of slavery within Africa.

5. T F The Albany Plan of Union brought most of the colonies together in 1754.
6. T F Sugar production was an important incentive to develop the transatlantic slave trade.
7. T F English growers in South Carolina taught African slaves how to plant and cultivate rice.
8. T F Some Africans in Virginia lived on an equal footing and intermarried with Europeans during the seventeenth century.
9. T F South Carolina planters spent summers closely supervising work in the rice fields.
10. T F New England's economy depended on selling food supplies for slaves in the West Indies.
11. T F Colonial slaveowners feared that Christianity would give their human property subversive ideas.
12. T F No established church was allowed in any North American colonies of Great Britain.
13. T F When tobacco prices declined, farmers in Virginia and Maryland planted wheat and corn.
14. T F A New England Congregationalist minister who displeased his flock invoked authority as God's representative to quell dissent.
15. T F The king of the Catawba tribe had marginal power, which he used mostly for negotiations with settlers.
16. T F Traders in South Carolina raped Indian women with impunity.
17. T F The Earl of Loudoun, commanding British forces in North America during the French and Indian War, inspired colonial support with his respect for local sentiments.
18. T F George Washington tried to become rich speculating in western lands.
19. T F Queen Anne's War fundamentally changed the relationship of Britain to its colonies.

G. MULTIPLE CHOICE—circle one or more correct answers.

1. Ships engaged in the transatlantic slave trade could be identified at sea or in port by
   a) the well-known "Jolly Roger" flag flying from the top of the mast.
   b) the often tell-tale shape of vessels constructed to hold human cargo.
   c) special licenses issued by the king of the country from which the ship sailed.
   d) the physical training on deck that slaves were put through to ready them for hard work.

2. Many people living in Africa who were sold as slaves had been
   a) lured aboard merchant ships with promises of good wages, then overpowered.
   b) captured in wars between African kingdoms, either soldiers or their dependents.
   c) living in isolated family groups that were vulnerable to kidnapping.
   d) singled out by their color as the most likely prospects to enslave.
   e) disoriented by the arrival of powerful European crews who disregarded local authority and laws.

3. Manners among the upper classes of colonial society
   a) excluded newly wealthy individuals from social acceptance in the upper classes.
   b) were defined by rules written down in "courtesy books."
   c) demanded that social graces in the parlor exclude all reference to useful activity.
   d) were designed to give offense to whoever was not part of the club.

4. The Catawba Indians of South Carolina
   a) were one of the oldest and well-established people in North America.
   b) were convenient to European colonists, who used them to guard the frontier.
   c) maintained strict racial and cultural purity and never intermarried with British colonials.
   d) fought alongside British troops and Tory militia during the American Revolution.
   e) were weakened in the 1750s by drought, smallpox, and settlers seeking their land.

5. The 1715 war between the Yamassee and South Carolina
   a) resulted from the enslavement of Yamassee by colonists for failure to pay debts.
   b) ended with the famous Battle of Fallen Timbers won by General Wayne.
   c) turned against the Yamassee when Captain George Chicken led a force of seventy Europeans and forty Africans to surprise a war party celebrating a previous victory.

d) was ended with the assistance of Iroquois sachems who negotiated a peace treaty.

e) created panic even in Charles Town for a few weeks while plantations were ravaged.

6. The average soldier in American colonial armies raised for the French and Indian War

   a) by his manner of fighting was responsible for adding the novel command "tree all!" to British military vocabulary.

   b) was a landless vagabond who enlisted in hope of getting a stake to acquire a farm.

   c) admired British gentleman officers and the disciplined maneuvers they led.

   d) simply was trying to get a job done so he could go home and live in safety.

   e) understood that the war would determine the kind of country he lived in.

7. Neolin, a Delaware visionary in a long line of prophets who arose among recently conquered Indian peoples,

   a) borrowed from Christian churches the use of wine for sacramental purposes.

   b) inspired the Ottawa chief Pontiac to begin an uprising against British rule.

   c) massacred a colony of Christian Indians known as the "Paxton Boys."

   d) saw his prophecies fulfilled by the peace that ended Indian uprisings in 1764.

   e) taught that all contact with Europeans must be ended, and called for relearning the art of making traditional weapons.

8. British forces took the city of Quebec from France in 1759 because

   a) Quebec's population was starved into surrender after a long siege.

   b) the British General James Wolfe learned of a footpath up a bluff from the St. Lawrence River to the Plains of Abraham west of the city.

   c) British soldiers learned to fire from ambush in the style of Indian warriors.

   d) an impulsive charge by French Canadian militia left the French line disorganized and vulnerable to British counterattack.

   e) Quebec's defenses were weak and its position near the river vulnerable.

9. The British Prime Minister William Pitt inspired colonial military support by

   a) proposing to grant the colonies autonomy from British imperial rule.

   b) reducing the authority of British officers to command higher-ranking officers of colonial provincial forces and militia.

   c) offering colonial troops the opportunity to loot and pillage Quebec and Montreal.

   d) bribing colonial governors to turn against the peaceful desires of the voters.

   e) recalling Lord Loudoun, and appealing to the colonies to raise military forces voluntarily in return for generous aid.

10. Conditions connected with the French and Indian War included

   a) attempts by Virginia land speculators, authorized by Lt. Gov. Dinwiddie, to establish a fort near present-day Pittsburgh on land claimed by France.

   b) anger that British colonial women, kidnapped by Indians, were being sold to a nunnery in Montreal.

   c) a blockade of the North American coast by French privateers.

   d) General Braddock's contemptuous refusal to guarantee Indian peoples continued occupancy of their traditional land in exchange for support in the war.

   e) competing claims by Virginia and Pennsylvania to the same territory.

H. ESSAY QUESTIONS OR ORAL REPORTS

   1. Identify three political or economic entities involved in the transatlantic slave trade, including any two that were European and another belonging to native Africans. Write one paragraph on each. Have a concluding paragraph on how the trade came to an end. Among possibilities to write about are Portugal, Holland, the Dutch West India Company, England, the Royal Africa Company, the Asante Union, the kingdom of Dahomey, the kingdom of Kongo, and the viceroyalty of New Spain.

2. Locate accounts of two or more revolts on board a transatlantic slave ship. Analyze how Africans sold into slavery might have had the social cohesion and coordination to attempt to seize a ship. Analyze the national origin and background of the crews of each ship. What determined the difference between successful and unsuccessful revolts?

3. How was the social status of slaves changed, from customs in the feudal societies of Africa to legal designation of slaves as property in the mercantile capitalist economy of the British empire? Document differences as to inheritance, rights and duties of master and slave, identification of slaves from the rest of the population. Make note of changes in the status of slaves in British North America between the early 1600s and the later 1700s.

4. Read John Woolman's journal, referenced on pages 107 and 108 of *This Land*, which is available in full on the Brandywine Press website. Why did Woolman, who was not a slave, address his employer as "master"? How did different individuals of the Quaker faith respond to the existence of slavery and ownership of slaves, within and without their own community?

5. Write an overview of the origins and growth patterns of the Great Awakening. Include any three denominations involved, and the responses of different classes and regions in colonial society. Also detail some major differences among any three of the most active individual preachers, in England and America, such as John Wesley, George Whitefield, Jonathan Edwards, William Tennent, James Davenport, Samuel Morris, William Robertson, and Samuel Davies.

6. Compare the survival strategies of the Yamassee and the Catawba in eighteenth-century South Carolina. What was the origin of each people? How successful was each in dealing with the Iroquois, with the South Carolina government, and with individual settlers living nearby? Choose one of the two and suggest how its survival strategies might have been improved.

British Blunders and American Rage

5

A. TERMS

Guy Fawkes Day _____
_____
_____

nonimportation _____
_____
_____

parliamentary representation _____
_____
_____

customs duties _____
_____
_____

impressment _____
_____
_____

committees of correspondence _____
_____
_____

Coercive Acts _____
_____
_____

natural rights _____
_____
_____

concept of liberty _____
_____
_____

"inalienable rights" _____
_____
_____

monarchy _____

_____

_____

B. PHOTOGRAPHS

1. Write about what a member of the mob on the left might be thinking. Then do the same for a poorly paid soldier in the line at the right.

_____

_____

_____

_____

_____

_____

_____

_____

_____

_____

_____

_____

_____

_____

_____

_____

_____

_____

_____

_____

_____

_____

_____

_____

_____

_____

_____

_____

_____

2. Why did African Americans in New England, such as the one pictured on the next page, generally enlist with patriot troops, while most blacks in the South who took up arms joined the British? To answer this question, look at the legal status, kinds of work, and relations with the rest of the community that shaped the lives of black northerners, and such conditions as they applied to African Americans in the South.

_____
_____
_____
_____
_____
_____
_____
_____
_____
_____
_____
_____
_____
_____
_____
_____
_____

_____
_____
_____
_____
_____
_____
_____
_____
_____
_____
_____
_____
_____
_____
_____
_____
_____
_____
_____
_____
_____
_____

C. VOCABULARY

press gangs _____

_____

_____

militia _____

_____

_____

Sons of Liberty _____

_____

_____

mob _____

_____

_____

tar and feather _____

_____

_____

vice-admiralty court _____

_____

_____

revenue _____

_____

_____

board of inquiry _____

_____

_____

D. INDIVIDUALS

George Grenville _____

_____

_____

Patrick Henry _____

_____

_____

James Otis _____

_____

_____

Phillis Wheatley _____

_____

_____

Daniel Dulany _____

_____

_____

Andrew Oliver _____

_____

_____

Ebenezer Macintosh _____

_____

Thomas Hutchinson _____

_____

Charles Townshend _____

_____

John Dickinson _____

_____

Samuel Adams _____

_____

John Hancock _____

_____

John Wilkes _____

_____

Captain Thomas Preston _____

_____

Christopher Gadsden _____

_____

Thomas Gage _____

_____

Thomas Paine _____

_____

Richard Henry Lee _____

_____

Thomas Jefferson _____

_____

E. FILL IN THE BLANKS.

In *Common Sense* (available on the Brandywine website) Thomas Paine wrote:

Everything that is _____
[high and holy / right or natural / pure or positive]

pleads for _____.
[separation / accord / reason and understanding / accommodation]

The blood of the slain, the _____
[wailing of our children / desperate calls of the captives / weeping voice of nature]

cries, _____.
[do not go gentle into that good night / we shall go down this road no more /
'tis time to part! / never again! / we have not yet begun to fight!]

F. TRUE FALSE—circle one.

1. T F Benjamin Franklin lobbied to have a business acquaintance appointed as a stamp agent.
2. T F Americans in the 1760s looked to the British monarch with loyalty and affection.
3. T F To the cheers of the mob, Thomas Hutchinson and the Boston sheriff evicted the stamp collection agent Andrew Oliver from his home.
4. T F James Otis argued that since colonists were not represented in Parliament, they had no legal right to object to taxes imposed by the British government.
5. T F Daniel Dulany argued that the British Parliament had the right to tax trade within the empire, while taxes on activity within a colony could be passed only by a body representative of the taxpayers.
6. T F The Sons of Liberty were a tightly disciplined conspiracy to overthrow British rule.
7. T F British merchants injured by the drop in exports to the colonies petitioned the government to repeal the Stamp Act.
8. T F The Whig party in British and colonial politics believed that the primary duty of subjects is to obey the commands of the government.
9. T F Many patriots believed that the liberty to own property without government interference included the right to property in slaves.
10. T F A larger part of the population could vote in America than in England, because property owning was a major qualification for voting and in British North America property in the form of land was widely available.
11. T F The Declaratory Act satisfied colonists that Parliament respected their rights.
12. T F The Townshend duties imposed a tax on imports of lead, paint, glass, paper, and tea.
13. T F All people in all the colonies had the same motives for hostility to the British government.
14. T F Artisans profited from the nonimportation agreements while merchants suffered a loss of business.
15. T F The Boston Tea Party was a response to Parliament's giving the British East India Company a monopoly.
16. T F British authorities tried to increase their control of the Massachusetts government by paying the governor and judges directly, instead of having the colonial legislature continue to pay the salaries.
17. T F The British schooner *Gaspée* was run aground by American customs officials policing the waters off Rhode Island.
18. T F British authorities decided to punish Massachusetts because it was the only colony where violent acts of resistance to the Tea Act had been committed.
19. T F Colonists objected to the Quebec Act because it granted religious tolerance to Roman Catholics in that province, a liberty many colonial Protestants opposed.
20. T F The British Parliament adopted a proposal to emancipate slaves throughout the colonies.
21. T F The Declaration of Independence warns that governments long established should not be changed for light or transient causes.
22. T F Colonists who supported the Revolution upheld the freedom of individuals to disagree with their neighbors.
23. T F Many educated people in the 1700s associated virtue with republicanism.

G. MULTIPLE CHOICE—circle one or more correct answers.

1. Among the forms of colonial resistance to the Stamp Act were
   a) closing down newspapers so that no taxable issues could be printed.
   b) hanging stamp agents in effigy and destroying their offices and homes.
   c) parades or dinners honoring stamp agents who refused their commissions.
   d) shooting at British soldiers from behind walls and trees.
   e) an embargo on all shipments of tobacco to England from the colonies.

2. The pamphlet entitled *Letters from a Pennsylvania Farmer*
   a) was a source of witty sayings and advice written by Benjamin Franklin.
   b) argued that Parliament could impose taxes only on imports.
   c) was published in serial form in 1767 and 1768 in Britain and the colonies.
   d) asserted that Parliament had no right to regulate trade with the colonies.
   e) sharpened familiar arguments that Parliament could not impose taxes to raise revenue on groups unrepresented in the House of Commons.

3. Motives for growing resistance to British rule in the colonies included
   a) anger among merchant seamen at impressment gangs that seized sailors for the Royal Navy.
   b) hostility to British soldiers off duty who took odd jobs in competition with colonists.
   c) fears among colonists that Roman Catholic refugees from Quebec would flood into the southern colonies.
   d) opposition to general warrants allowing searches of homes on any suspicion.
   e) indignation among American merchants who had grown rich smuggling goods without paying a tax and resented the attempts of customs officers to crack down.

4. The Boston Massacre was a confrontation that escalated from incidents that included
   a) a fight between several soldiers and a rope maker and his friends over a perceived insult in an offer of employment cleaning an outhouse.
   b) several gunnings of civilians on Boston Commons by bands of British troops.
   c) snipings at soldiers on sentry duty.
   d) confiscation by British search parties of Paul Revere's subversive silver engravings.
   e) assaults on a sentry after he clubbed an apprentice who had been baiting him.

5. The measures approved at the first meeting of the Continental Congress included
   a) the Declaration of Independence of the United States from Great Britain.
   b) prohibitions on exports to Britain and imports from the home country.
   c) gradual manumission of slaves in all thirteen colonies.
   d) the Suffolk Resolves, declaring the Coercive Acts unconstitutional and urging Massachusetts to resist British policy.
   e) bans on horse racing, cockfights, theater, tea drinking, and luxurious dress.

6. Although the Continental Congress had no legal authority, its decisions were enforced
   a) through signed contracts and covenants enforceable in most colonial courts.
   b) by committees of local patriots under an association formed by the Continental Congress.
   c) by the authority of British army commanders sympathetic to colonial demands.
   d) by shunning and boycott of the businesses of whoever did not cooperate.
   e) under threats to tar and feather violators of the regulations of Congress.

7. The Continental Congress acted in the manner of a sovereign people, not subjects, when
   a) it voted to open American ports to all nations except for Great Britain.
   b) appeals were addressed to King George to rein in the excesses of Parliament.
   c) Thomas Paine blamed the king for British government policies.
   d) Silas Deane was appointed to purchase arms and ammunition in Europe.
   e) the Olive Branch Petition asked Parliament for amicable terms of settlement.

8. Among the reasons one third of the colonists remained loyal to Great Britain were
   a) a belief that established laws should not be recklessly overthrown.
   b) a desire to speculate in western lands and remove Indian peoples from them.
   c) ownership of large estates, which distinguished them from the rabble in arms.
   d) an emotional attachment to king and empire that they were unwilling to break.
   e) certainty that the rights of Englishmen were best preserved by royal rule.

9. Lord North's final proposal to Parliament before open hostilities broke out in the colonies
   a) required that all members of the Continental Congress go into exile for five years.
   b) recognized the Continental Congress and gave the colonies a voice in revenue.
   c) went nowhere because King George wanted to reassert government authority.
   d) was defeated by the strenuous opposition of the aging William Pitt.
   e) proposed to appease colonists by restoring the Stuart dynasty to the throne.

10. Residents of the colony of Georgia sought legalization of slavery because
    a) they believed that since slaves were property, and liberty was founded on property, denying them the ownership of slaves violated liberty.
    b) only wealthy landowners had been allowed to emigrate to Georgia.
    c) neighboring Spanish Florida had large numbers of slaves working in its fields.
    d) church attendance was low, and it was expected that slaves would rapidly convert.
    e) rice became a chief crop, and the need for slave labor overcame the trustees' original vision of creating a virtuous society.

H. ESSAY QUESTIONS OR ORAL REPORTS

1. Examine the social and political role of the crowd in Boston, and make some brief comparisons with social classes and customs in one of these colonies: New York, Pennsylvania, Virginia, or South Carolina. Look up information on daily and annual events in the 1760s, not just political upheaval. Guy Fawkes Day is but one example.

2. What were the origins and the practices of the militia in colonial America? To what extent were the militia prescribed in royal charters and orders prepared by companies that financed early colonization? To what extent was the militia a response to practical necessities in America? Why and how did reliance on the militia act as a brake on unpopular government measures? How did reliance on militia forces allow prejudice and hysteria to rule at times? Include the Regulators in South Carolina. Analyze how the colonial experience of the militia contributed to the adoption of the Second Amendment to the United States Constitution, and, since this is a subject which historians debate fiercely, document your position.

3. How would the Tea Act have been received by various classes and regions in colonial America if a high level of resentment did not already exist against the British government? Who would have benefited from the cheap availability of tea? Who would have suffered? This requires looking up some data on production and import of goods, on what household goods different classes typically bought, on who imported and sold teas, legally or by smuggling. How might colonial society have lined up politically if tea had really been the only issue?

4. Look into the details of the Coercive Acts. Locate the actual language of each. Did they violate any rights already established in British law at the time? Did they, in any case, violate rights the colonists had come to expect in practice? Did the actual execution of the acts, by British authorities in the colonies, exceed the authority they had been given by Parliament?

5. What were the military strengths and weaknesses of the regular British army, the militia assembled at Lexington and Concord, and what became the Continental Army under George Washington? Go beyond platitudes about discipline and precision on one side, and passionate devotion to home and country on the other, although both may have a part in your analysis. Examine at least some of these factors: training, experience, motivation, or the lack of it,

turnover in the ranks, crass self-interest on both sides, and internal conflicts within each army. Make reference to why each side won or lost significant battles. Look also at alliances and agreements, both with Indian nations and with European countries.

_____

_____

_____

_____

_____

_____

_____

_____

_____

_____

_____

_____

_____

_____

_____

_____

_____

_____

_____

_____

_____

_____

_____

_____

_____

_____

_____

_____

_____

_____

_____

_____

_____

Winning Independence

6

A. TERMS

constitutional monarch _____
_____
_____

Hessians _____
_____
_____

assessed value of property _____
_____
_____

Constitution _____
_____
_____

republic _____
_____
_____

civic virtue _____
_____
_____

inflationary spiral _____
_____
_____

Continental dollar _____
_____
_____

guerrilla warfare _____
_____
_____

national domain _____
_____
_____

femme covert _____

_____

_____

emancipation _____

_____

_____

civilian supremacy _____

_____

_____

public debt _____

_____

_____

subsistence farming _____

_____

_____

B. PHOTOGRAPHS

Write a summary of the demographic character of the troops who fought for American independence. What motivated the different social and economic classes that joined the struggle for independence?

_____
_____
_____
_____
_____
_____
_____
_____
_____
_____
_____
_____
_____
_____
_____
_____
_____
_____
_____
_____
_____
_____
_____

C. VOCABULARY

the crowd _____
_____
_____

tyrant _____
_____
_____

guillotine _____

_____

_____

mercenaries _____

_____

_____

summer soldiers and sunshine patriots _____

_____

_____

duties _____

_____

_____

estuaries _____

_____

_____

loyalists _____

_____

_____

Articles of Confederation _____

_____

_____

cession _____

_____

_____

squatters _____

_____

_____

mutiny _____

_____

_____

currency _____

_____

_____

D. INDIVIDUALS

King George III _____

_____

King Louis XVI (France) _____

_____

_____

Lord North _____

_____

John Burgoyne _____

_____

Philip Schuyler _____

_____

Horatio Gates _____

_____

Beaumarchais _____

_____

Arthur Lee _____

_____

Marquis de Lafayette _____

_____

Thaddeus Kosciuszko _____

_____

Comte de Vergennes _____

_____

Friedrich von Steuben _____

_____

Lord Cornwallis _____

_____

George Washington _____

_____

Francis Marion _____

_____

_____

Henry Clinton _____

_____

Benedict Arnold _____

_____

John André _____

_____

Comte de Rochambeau _____

_____

Admiral de Grasse _____

_____

Alexander Hamilton _____

_____

John Jay _____

_____

John Adams _____

_____

Nathanael Greene _____

_____

James Madison _____

_____

Joseph Brant _____

_____

Daniel Shays _____

_____

Benjamin Lincoln _____

_____

E. FILL IN THE BLANKS.

In *The American Crisis* Thomas Paine wrote:

These are the times that _____.
[fry men's soles / take their tolls / test our goals / try men's souls / thin the rolls / defy all polls]

The summer soldier and the _____
[winter soldier / friend of freedom / southern aristocrat / sunshine patriot / autumn coward]

will, in this crisis, shrink from the _____;
[task at hand / prospect of democracy / service of his country]

but he that stands it NOW, deserves _____.
[the parades and honors that will follow our victory / the love and thanks of man and woman /
to be remembered proudly for all time / the grant of land to be given them after the war]

Write a paragraph explaining the reasons for Paine's issuing the pamphlet when he did, and make clear what he was arguing for. The essay can be found on www.brandywinesources.com

_____

_____

_____

_____

_____

_____

_____

_____

_____

_____

_____

_____

_____

_____

_____

_____

_____

F. TRUE FALSE—circle one.

1. T F The largest number of casualties in the invasion of Quebec by the rebels was inflicted on both armies by smallpox.
2. T F George Washington secured a series of brilliant victories in 1776, driving the British out of New York and Long Island.
3. T F In the winter of 1777, rebel leaders worried about the disaffection of colonial civilians from the cause of independence.
4. T F The difficulty of moving troops through the great stretches of the inland hampered British efforts to retake the North American colonies.
5. T F The Howe brothers' authority to negotiate peace with Continental forces was limited to offering pardons and conveying American grievances to the British government.
6. T F Many upper-class Philadelphians welcomed British occupation and the elegant social season made possible by the presence of young British officers.
7. T F France, still angry over losing Quebec in the French and Indian War, refused to give any aid to the American colonies in their struggle for independence.

8.   T   F   The unaided victory of the Continental Army over a polished professional military force was a triumph of American individualism over European military tradition.

9.   T   F   Colonial victory over the British at Saratoga persuaded France to enter the war against Britain.

10.   T   F   The Articles of Confederation were unanimously adopted by all thirteen states in 1778.

11.   T   F   State constitutions written during the American Revolution extended the right to vote to all men in every state.

12.   T   F   The War for Independence required taxes heavier than people had previously known.

13.   T   F   Merchants and planters in Charles Town, South Carolina, fearing damage to their elegant homes, urged General Benjamin Lincoln to surrender the city to the British.

14.   T   F   Daniel Morgan had confidence that the militia he commanded would stand firm in the face of enemy fire and not run away.

15.   T   F   With Cornwallis's surrender in 1781, all British forces immediately returned to England.

16.   T   F   On June 4, 1781, Cornwallis's troops nearly captured Virginia Governor Thomas Jefferson at his hilltop estate near Charlottesville.

17.   T   F   Peace with Great Britain motivated every colony to put aside its own interests.

18.   T   F   After the Revolution, New York hoped to recover control of Vermont.

19.   T   F   Quakers and Baptists were the primary denominations morally opposed to slavery.

20.   T   F   Benedict Arnold had a reputation as an audacious and clever American commander.

21.   T   F   American merchants patriotically kept prices low throughout the Revolutionary War.

22.   T   F   Congress under the Articles of Confederation made decisions by majority vote of all delegates present.

G. MULTIPLE CHOICE—circle one or more correct answers.

1. British strategy at the beginning of the War for Independence
    a) focused on crushing resistance in New England, the seedbed of rebellion.
    b) attempted first to seize the capitals of every colony, then to move into the interior.
    c) began with the recapture of Nova Scotia from rebellious colonists.
    d) relied on offering generous terms to settle colonial grievances.
    e) suffered from a shortage of manpower to secure New England.

2. By December 1776, British armies in North America had
    a) lost control of all fortifications in the thirteen colonies to the Continental Army.
    b) secured control of New York City and all fortified positions in the vicinity.
    c) implemented a scorched earth policy to terrify the colonies into surrender.
    d) occupied Rhode Island and a large part of New Jersey.
    e) proclaimed general emancipation of all slaves in colonies then in rebellion.

3. Between Christmas 1776 and New Year's Day 1777, General Washington's army
    a) drove Hessian mercenaries out of New York City, retaking it for revolutionary forces.
    b) conducted a raid across the Delaware River, surprising Hessian troops at Trenton.
    c) picked off a British garrison at Princeton.
    d) abandoned Philadelphia, which became a British stronghold thereafter.
    e) forced Gen. Howe to regroup his army around New York.

4. Prior to the American victory at Saratoga, French aid consisted of
    a) diplomatic requests to Great Britain to accept American independence.
    b) funds and supplies funneled clandestinely to colonial forces.
    c) preparations for an uprising in Quebec to restore French rule.
    d) assistance provided through a trading company directed by the playwright Beaumarchais.

5. When Patrick Henry proposed public financing for all Christian ministers in Virginia,
    a) George Washington and Thomas Jefferson rallied support for the idea.
    b) the state's growing community of Baptists objected, holding that all churches should depend on the voluntary support of their members.

c) petitions by James Madison and others, signed by ten thousand, opposed the measure.

d) Roman Catholic bishops objected to the payment of tax money to Protestant ministers.

e) Bill 82 was quickly passed, ending all public support for religion in Virginia.

6. The uprising of Massachusetts farmers, led by Captain Daniel Shays, was
   a) a widely misunderstood peaceful protest against government policy.
   b) a response by farmers to the threat of losing their land for an inability to pay taxes and private debts.
   c) a terrorist conspiracy threatening to destroy all law and order in the state.
   d) partly inspired by the scarcity of cash among farmers to pay taxes with.
   e) an application of tactics used against British authority before the Revolution.

7. James Madison concluded that the government under the Articles of Confederation
   a) took too much power from the states, and had to be brought under control.
   b) could not function insofar as amendments required unanimous approval of all states.
   c) should be replaced with a government having authority to pass laws that operated directly on the citizenry, not merely through the states.
   d) worked well to restrain the natural tendency of government to become tyrannical.
   e) had ruined the American economy by imposing high rates of taxation.

8. The convention that eventually wrote the United States Constitution
   a) was called for that purpose by an invitation circulated to all state legislatures.
   b) assembled in response to a decree from George Washington.
   c) was suggested at a meeting of delegates from five states to discuss commerce.
   d) resulted from demands for an overhaul of Congress.
   e) assembled in response to an invitation issued with no certainty as to how well it would be attended.

9. Among the competing regional interests dividing Americans after independence were
   a) New England states that cared more about fishing off Newfoundland than about navigation on the Mississippi River.
   b) southern states that wanted to give all land north of the Ohio back to Canada once the Northwest Ordinance banned slavery in that region.
   c) New York's wealthy patroons, who proposed an alliance with Quebec against the more democratic New England farmers.
   d) southern planters who preferred to import luxuries from England and sell their crops there, not deal with sharp-eyed New England merchants and manufacturers.
   e) merchants in port cities like Philadelphia and New York who saw merchants in cities other than their own as commercial rivals more than part of one national economy.

10. Among the incidents that showed how limited the authority of the Continental Congress remained were these:
    a) Money could not be obtained from the states to pay financial obligations.
    b) Representatives traveling to Philadelphia were routinely chased and robbed.
    c) Continental army officers talked of mutiny over the failure of Congress to pay pensions.
    d) Maryland, Delaware, and New Jersey refused to allow delegates to cross their territory on the way to meetings of Congress.
    e) Unpaid soldiers surrounded the statehouse in Philadelphia where Congress was meeting, and local authorities refused to disperse them.

H. ESSAY QUESTIONS OR ORAL REPORTS

1. Write a leaflet to be distributed by British forces in New England, to regain the loyalty and support of the population, taking it away from the Continental Congress, its army, and revolutionary state legislatures. Consider carefully what interests in the civilian population to appeal to, and how to drive a wedge dividing these interests from the cause of independence. Choose

an appropriate mix of threats and concessions. Then write one leaflet for use by the rebels to counter the British campaign. Write a one- or two-page overview explaining your choices.

2. Read the full text of Thomas Paine's pamphlet *The American Crisis* (available on www.brandywinesources.com). What does it say about the desirability of peace and the necessity of war? Would Paine have extended the same analysis to a war between established nations?

3. Were William and Richard Howe grossly incompetent and lazy, were they attempting to sabotage the British war effort because they supported the opposition party in the British Parliament, or were they simply attempting the impossible task of reestablishing government authority without alienating the colonists? All three views can be found in historical sources. Document the conclusions you draw after reading them.

4. What strategy might have brought success to General Burgoyne's 1777 campaign (which in real life ended in disaster with the American victory at Saratoga)? How would this alternate strategy improve Burgoyne's speed of movement? Could more support have been won from loyalist and undecided colonials? How could Continental forces have been divided from one another? How could forces from New York have better aided Burgoyne?

5. Find and review the language of two or three state constitutions adopted between 1776 and 1790. Many of these are available from web sources, as well as in state histories in the library. Identify some common themes that make them different from constitutions in these same states today. How do the eighteenth-century constitutions of your choosing differ from one another?

6. Read the Articles of Confederation, and analyze the strengths and weaknesses of the document as a basis for national government. Could the United States have remained united at all under the Articles? How would the Civil War or World War II have been handled under a Confederation government?

7. Summarize the causes of Shays's Rebellion, and the role of various units of the state militia in suppressing it. What political divides separated legislators representing the wealthy Boston area from legislators speaking for farmers in western Massachusetts? How unequal were eastern and western Massachusetts in their ability to pay property taxes in hard money? What effect did the rebellion have on the next statewide election? Were grievances among farmers about foreclosure actually alleviated?

8. In what ways that had not been predicted or originally intended were the thirteen colonies transformed through the War for Independence? Consider the rights, liberties, and obligations of citizenship as colonial critics of Britain described them before the Revolution and as they actually came to exist in the years after independence was secured. Who became rich during the Revolution, and who impoverished?

Constituting the National Republic

7

A. TERMS

judicial review _____
_____
_____

enumerated powers _____
_____
_____

interstate commerce _____
_____
_____

sedition _____
_____
_____

branches of government _____
_____
_____

Anti-Federalists _____
_____
_____

supreme law of the land _____
_____
_____

import duties _____
_____
_____

excise tax _____
_____
_____

B. PHOTOGRAPHS

When Alexander Hamilton drafted John Jay's instructions for negotiations with Britain over trade, land, and financial disputes, then leaked them to the British minister to the United States, did he commit an act of espionage or treason? Or compare Jay's view in *The Federalist* number 64 on the character of society and government with Hamilton's as he formulated it while secretary of the treasury.

_____

_____

_____

_____

_____

_____

_____

_____

_____

_____

_____

_____

_____

_____

_____

_____

_____

C. VOCABULARY

apportionment _____
_____
_____

constituents _____
_____
_____

executive _____
_____
_____

judiciary _____
_____
_____

ratification _____
_____
_____

sovereignty _____
_____
_____

Potomac River _____
_____
_____

federal system _____
_____
_____

Girondins _____
_____
_____

Jacobins _____
_____
_____

neutrality _____
_____
_____

faction _____
_____
_____

blockade _____
_____
_____

D. INDIVIDUALS

Martha Washington _____

_____

_____

Martha Ballard _____

_____

Edmund Randolph _____

_____

George Mason _____

_____

John Singleton Copley _____

_____

Abigail Adams _____

_____

James Madison _____

_____

Aaron Burr _____

_____

Oliver Ellsworth _____

_____

Charles Cotesworth Pinckney _____

_____

X, Y, and Z _____

_____

John Fenno _____

_____

Philip Freneau _____

_____

George Clinton _____
_____
_____

John Marshall _____
_____
_____

Edmond Genêt _____
_____
_____

Elbridge Gerry _____
_____
_____

Thomas Pinckney _____
_____
_____

Timothy Pickering _____
_____
_____

Talleyrand _____
_____
_____

Matthew Lyon _____
_____
_____

E. FILL IN THE BLANKS.

Fill in the blanks in Abigail Adams's challenge to her husband John Adams.

Do not put such unlimited _____
[faith / revenue / power / rhetoric / vision]
into the hands of _____.
[clergy / husbands / bureaucrats / fanatics / merchants]
Remember all _____ would be _____ if they could.
[women*lawyers / housewives*schoolteachers / kings*soldiers / men*tyrants / ladies*artists]
If particular care and attention is not _____
[given to the wealthy / devoted to the household / paid to the ladies / expended on the furniture]
we are determined to _____
[withdraw to the kitchen / foment a rebellion / establish our own clubs / plead for redress]
and will not hold ourselves _____
[subject to any authority / in waiting for a festival / devoted to traditions / bound by any laws]
in which we have no voice.

F. TRUE FALSE—circle one.

1. T F All thirteen original states were represented at the Constitutional Convention.
2. T F The executive branch of government was originally considered one of the weak branches.

3.   T   F   When the Constitution was ratified, New York City was the national capital.

4.   T   F   Madison tried to persuade the House of Representatives that original holders of the national debt should be paid in full, and later purchasers should receive less.

5.   T   F   Alexander Hamilton was concerned with constructing a government well balanced among the different branches, and with reconciling the doubts of Anti-Federalists.

6.   T   F   In the early 1800s, New England newlyweds took several weeks after the wedding setting up their own house and moving into it.

7.   T   F   At the turn of the nineteenth century, New England marriages were an important church ritual.

8.   T   F   Jefferson, Madison, and Hamilton found that since the Constitution empowered Congress to collect taxes and pay debts, Congress had the constitutional authority to charter a national bank.

9.   T   F   The federal Constitution envisioned elections between two competing national parties.

10.   T   F   An early episode in the creation of political parties was the dispute over Hamilton's program.

11.   T   F   Hamilton's praise of the British government later persuaded Madison that Hamilton was a closet monarchist, not a republican.

12.   T   F   A general war in Europe in 1793 threatened disaster to American farmers and merchants.

13.   T   F   When John Adams proposed to address the President as "His Highness," critics began referring to the well-rounded Adams as "His Rotundity."

14.   T   F   When the French diplomat Edmond Genêt was recalled for probable arrest and execution, he stayed in the United States and married the daughter of Governor George Clinton of New York.

15.   T   F   The Philadelphia physician Benjamin Rush proved in 1793 that African Americans were immune to yellow fever.

16.   T   F   Indians in the Ohio Valley inflicted heavy casualties on United States military forces in 1790 and 1791.

17.   T   F   Jefferson and Adams were lifelong political opponents who never ceased resenting each other.

18.   T   F   The Reign of Terror in the French Revolution was ended when a new government took power that was more friendly to the United States.

19.   T   F   At the time of the XYZ Affair, the French foreign minister Talleyrand had just returned from two years living in exile in the United States.

20.   T   F   In the first several presidential elections, many members of the Electoral College were appointed by decision of the state legislature without a popular vote.

21.   T   F   All the delegates to the convention that produced the federal Constitution took an active part in the four months of daily debate.

22.   T   F   As a compromise between large and small states, the Constitution assigned the Senate sole responsibility for initiating revenue bills.

23.   T   F   Nine ratifying states could have formed a federal government under the new Constitution, while the states not ratifying would have remained independent of it.

24.   T   F   In Rhode Island, only a popular referendum secured ratification of the Constitution.

25.   T   F   For the first several decades, federal revenue came mostly from collecting import duties.

G. MULTIPLE CHOICE—circle one or more correct answers.

1. Modes for election of the president considered by the Constitutional Convention included
   a) installing as president each year the man who made the largest voluntary contribution to paying the expenses of government.
   b) direct election by the people of all the states.
   c) election by the national legislature for a single lengthy term.
   d) appointment by the Supreme Court of a president who would serve for life.
   e) use of electors selected by each state to choose the president.

2. Madison opposed Hamilton's plan to pay off all war debts at full value because
   a) they had been political enemies for years.
   b) Virginia planters were afraid their property would be taxed to pay off new bonds.

c) speculators had bought up much of the debt at huge discounts from veterans and others; paying it at full value would give these speculators a huge profit.

d) Madison believed the government should just print more money as needed.

e) assuming state debt would reward states that had not paid their own obligations, at the expense of states that had already paid theirs.

3. Among the names applied to the emerging political parties in the 1790s were
   a) "Monocrats" and "Anglomans," applied to Hamiltonians by their opponents.
   b) "Democratic" or "Republican," as Madison's followers called themselves.
   c) "Germans," "Huns," and "Communists," as all factions called one another.
   d) "Glorious Knights of Saint Tammany," a third newly formed party.
   e) "Democrats," "Jacobins," and "Gallomans," as Federalists called their opponents.

4. As a result of John Jay's negotiations with British diplomats in 1794 and 1795,
   a) American merchant shipping was guaranteed access to West Indian ports.
   b) fearing an American alliance with France, Britain withdrew all claims against the United States and against American citizens.
   c) Britain agreed to relinquish western forts and establish arbitration commissions.
   d) France declared war on the United States.
   e) a storm of political protest swept the country when the terms were publicized.

5. In the first contested presidential election, that of 1796,
   a) no candidate received a majority in the Electoral College.
   b) John Adams was elected the second president.
   c) Aaron Burr and Alexander Hamilton ran against each other for vice president.
   d) all candidates addressed huge rallies for months before the election.
   e) Hamilton tried to manipulate voting in the Electoral College so that Thomas Pinckney would become president instead of Adams.

6. The XYZ Affair early in John Adams's administration was
   a) a scientific experiment in genetics conducted by Benjamin Franklin in Paris.
   b) probably arranged by British agents to drive the United States into war with France.
   c) the result of a diplomatic mission to France by John Marshall, Charles Cotesworth Pinckney, and Elbridge Gerry.
   d) a label that was attached to a demand by three agents of the French foreign minister Talleyrand for a substantial loan to France and a large bribe.
   e) an attempt by the French mathematician René Descartes to chart his country's relations with the United States on a graph.

7. The army assembled in response to the XYZ Affair could not be used against France,
   a) but Adams secretly intended to send it to Canada and declare war against Britain.
   b) so Republicans suspected it was really intended for use in suppressing domestic opposition to the Federalists.
   c) since any expeditionary force from France would risk attack by the British navy.
   d) and Hamilton staffed its officer corps with loyal Federalists, creating suspicion he would like to march it through states dominated by Republicans.
   e) so Congress quickly repealed the funding authorization to maintain it.

8. Among the many attempts to manipulate the outcome of the 1800 presidential election, the only tactic NOT used was
   a) an effort by Alexander Hamilton in New York to replace election of a single slate by the legislature with voting by district, to salvage some Federalist electors.

b) Virginia's decision to adopt a statewide winner-take-all election, denying the Federalist Party an electoral vote from the Richmond area.

c) a decision by Massachusetts to abandon district voting and choose electors on a statewide basis, to prevent election of a minority of Republican electors.

d) deploying at the polls in several states a body of armed Regulators, who would watch people mark their ballots and arrest, beat, or kill opposition voters.

e) Alexander Hamilton's scheme to throw the votes of Federalist electors to his preferred candidate, Charles Pinckney, rather than the incumbent John Adams.

9. In the course of the arguments over ratification of the Constitution,
   a) armed uprisings in five states attempted to prevent imposition of federal authority.
   b) Patrick Henry delivered three weeks of impassioned denunciations of the proposed scheme of government.
   c) Alexander Hamilton tried to impose ratification by a coup d'état.
   d) a popular referendum in Rhode Island rejected the Constitution outright.
   e) a state convention in North Carolina rejected the Constitution.

H. ESSAY QUESTIONS OR ORAL REPORTS

1. What does the debate about counting slaves, for purposes of congressional representation, reveal about the understanding of elected representation at the time the Constitution was written? To answer this question, look at South Carolina and at one northern state, and for each of the two consider the right to vote, and what portion was excluded. Property, gender, nationality, race are all factors to be considered. Also consider South Carolina's state constitution requiring that members of the upper house of the legislature own a number of slaves.

2. Analyze Madison's view that the primary danger to the rights of individuals would lie within the states, where popular majorities could impose unjust laws. Give some historical examples that support this view. Give some instances in which states protected the rights of individuals in the face of federal violations. For this you might want to look up the measures some northern states adopted in the years prior to the Civil War protecting against federal fugitive slave laws the slaves who had fled to the North, and protecting against federal punishment whoever aided the fugitives.

3. Choose Madison, Hamilton, or another major personality in the early years of American politics whose views you agree with or at least find it worthwhile to explore. Explain briefly what classes or interests in American society the political figure of your choice would have thought to be most important to strengthen, and which most necessary to restrain. Lay out your own program for the economic and political foundations of the federal government. Draw on programs proposed at the time, but use the benefit of hindsight to make your own improvements.

4. Compare with attitudes in the restless colonies toward British government authority some responses to the exercise of authority by the newly established federal government. How did the philosophies that sustained a revolt make it difficult to establish a new authority? How did the necessities of winning a revolution require effective government? Suggest how the attitudes apparent in events at that time still manifest themselves in American society today.

5. Review the opportunities and dangers that came with American policy toward Britain and France between 1789 and 1800. What were the advantages to the United States of being close to either one? What were the liabilities? What were the advantages, and realistic possibilities, of remaining neutral?

6. Look up and read the original text of the Alien and Sedition Acts. State and explain your own analysis as to whether these acts violated the Constitution, and if so, whose job it was to invalidate them after their adoption by Congress. Compare these laws with other acts of the same or similar names passed during World War I and subsequently. Is there any validity to the largely

discredited belief that states have the authority to act as a check on unconstitutional acts by the federal government?

_____

_____

_____

_____

_____

_____

_____

_____

_____

_____

_____

_____

_____

_____

_____

_____

_____

_____

_____

_____

_____

_____

_____

_____

_____

_____

_____

_____

_____

_____

_____

_____

_____

_____

_____

_____

Jefferson and His Agricultural Republic

8

A. TERMS

paper blockade _____
_____
_____

Marshall Court _____
_____
_____

embargo _____
_____
_____

orders-in-council _____
_____
_____

War Hawks _____
_____
_____

standing armies _____
_____
_____

right of deposit _____
_____
_____

national debt _____
_____
_____

civil liberties _____
_____
_____

freedom of the seas _____
_____
_____

officer corps _____

central banking _____

B. VOCABULARY

inauguration _____

tributaries (rivers) _____

levees _____

patronage _____

impeachment _____

lucrative _____

duel _____

corsairs _____

deserters _____

consul _____

annihilate _____

West Point _____

_____

arbitration _____

_____

squadron _____

_____

demilitarize _____

_____

amphibious military force _____

_____

C. INDIVIDUALS

Meriwether Lewis _____

_____

William Clark _____

_____

Sacajawea _____

_____

Albert Gallatin _____

_____

Little Turtle _____

_____

Anthony Wayne _____

_____

John Marshall _____

_____

Eli Whitney _____

_____

James Wilkinson _____

_____

_____

William Marbury _____

_____

_____

David Erskine _____

_____

_____

Tecumseh _____

_____

_____

Tenskwatawa _____

_____

_____

Henry Clay _____

_____

_____

Isaac Hull _____

_____

_____

Oliver Hazard Perry _____

_____

_____

Thomas MacDonough _____

_____

_____

Stephen Decatur _____

_____

_____

D. TRUE FALSE—circle one.

1. T F President Thomas Jefferson suspected that wooly mammoths might still live in the vast unexplored territory of the Louisiana Purchase.
2. T F Political campaigns at the turn of the nineteenth century were fierce public events that tore communities apart with several months of mass meetings and campaign speeches.
3. T F In 1800, most of the sixteen states chose presidential electors by majority vote of the state legislature.
4. T F Thomas Jefferson remarked that "A little revolution every twenty years is an excellent thing."
5. T F By 1800 conservation of dwindling forests had become important to most Americans.
6. T F German immigrants were conspicuously wasteful of natural resources.
7. T F In 1800 New York and Philadelphia were the only American cities with more than sixty thousand residents.
8. T F Ships traveling by river from New York to Albany boasted a regular sailing schedule.

9. T F Thomas Jefferson ran up a large national debt, spending the Treasury surplus generated by the policies of Alexander Hamilton.

10. T F Federalists on the Supreme Court set judicial precedents upholding freedom of the press by overturning convictions of Federalist editors charged with seditious libel by Pierpoint Edwards, Jefferson's appointee as United States attorney for Connecticut.

11. T F President Thomas Jefferson was a close and lasting friend of his distant cousin, John Marshall, chief justice of the United States.

12. T F General Arthur St. Clair won a decisive victory over the Miami under Little Turtle in 1791 in a battle at the Wabash River.

13. T F Thomas Jefferson viewed the conflict between Indians and people of European descent as a contest between savagery and civilization.

14. T F By the time Jefferson left office, the federal government had acquired two hundred thousand more acres of land from Indians, most of it along the Ohio and Mississippi rivers.

15. T F In 1803 the United States acquired an enormous stretch of territory from France..

16. T F Thomas Jefferson referred to the Louisiana Purchase as "an empire for liberty."

17. T F Free African Americans in 1800 worked as sailors, shipbuilders, barbers, tailors, carpenters, masons, and innkeepers.

18. T F Jefferson and Madison were confident that newly freed slaves could be absorbed easily into the general society of Virginia.

19. T F Aaron Burr was vice president of the United States when he shot Alexander Hamilton in a duel in New Jersey.

20. T F The United States was commercially self-sufficient and independent of European powers across the Atlantic Ocean.

21. T F Napoleon's Berlin Decree and a British order-in-council of 1806 guaranteed freedom of the seas to neutral ships trading with the opposing side.

22. T F By 1810 over one million settlers lived west of the Appalachian Mountains.

23. T F Tecumseh played a part alongside regular British army troops in defeating the first invasion of Canada and taking Detroit from the United States.

24. T F William Harrison established a defensive line in the War of 1812 that effectively surrendered a large part of the northwestern United States to the enemy.

25. T F The U.S.S. *Constitution* was named "Old Ironsides" because it was the first ship to have its hull protected by steel plates.

26. T F Creek Indians killed 250 militia soldiers under Andrew Jackson at the battle of Horseshoe Bend on the Alabama River.

27. T F At the 1814 Hartford Convention, New Englanders discussed secession from the Union.

28. T F The 1817 Rush-Bagot Treaty created the longest unfortified national border in the world.

29. T F United States forces refused to give up the nation's capital to the invading British army.

30. T F In September 1814, British hopes of taking Baltimore were repulsed.

31. T F The Treaty of Ghent, ending the War of 1812, secured satisfaction of all American grievances against Britain, particularly concerning impressment and rights of neutral shipping.

E. MULTIPLE CHOICE—circle one or more correct answers.

1. The population of the United States in 1800 according to the census included
   a) just over fifty million people concentrated along the Mississippi and Great Lakes.
   b) about twenty percent of known African descent, most of them slaves.
   c) an equal division between speakers of English, German, French, and Spanish.
   d) a labor force concentrated mostly in cities like Boston and New York.
   e) an average of 6.1 inhabitants per square mile, not counting Native Americans.

2. In 1800 the United States was self-sufficient in agriculture, an economic sector that also
   a) exported cotton and rubber to Europe and Asia.
   b) shipped grain, beef, pork, tobacco, fish, and rice all over the world.
   c) sold a large surplus to feed the sugar plantations in the West Indies.

d) sent superior kinds of whiskey to Scotland, wines to France, and brandy to Spain.

e) provided a livelihood for the great majority of American workers.

3. Travel in the United States in 1800 typically included
   a) a three-day trip by stagecoach from New York to Boston three times a week.
   b) two days for a ninety-mile stagecoach trip from Philadelphia to New York.
   c) moving goods and people by water wherever that was possible.
   d) high speed horse relays covering the length of the nation in five days.
   e) brutality, negligence, and filching, which regular travelers had come to expect.

4. Thomas Jefferson changed the federal government in Washington by
   a) tearing down partly completed marble buildings in favor of a log cabin style.
   b) ending formal banquets that he considered trappings of monarchy.
   c) decreeing freedom of all slaves in the District of Columbia, and to set an example, freeing those who worked for him at Monticello.
   d) holding small informal meetings at the Executive Mansion with citizens, diplomats, and members of Congress.
   e) sending written messages to Congress rather than appearing in person to speak.

5. Republicans resented John Adams's last-minute appointment of new federal judges and
   a) had all the appointees arrested for an indefinite period of time.
   b) created a new set of courts that competed with the courts filled by Federalists.
   c) abolished most of the new positions as wasteful, repealing the laws that had created them.
   d) announced that no ruling by a Federalist judge would be enforced.
   e) authorized state legislatures to nullify decisions by federal judges in their state.

6. Napoleon was willing to sell Louisiana to the United States because
   a) Spain refused to turn over Mexico to France, so Louisiana alone was not worth it.
   b) he hoped to win over the United States as an ally in his wars against Britain.
   c) the army Napoleon had sent to regain St. Domingue as a colony was being defeated.
   d) Napoleon's plans for Louisiana had been based on having control of the wealthy sugar plantations of St. Domingue.

7. Among the effects that war between Britain and France brought to neutral shipping were these:
   a) Civilian merchant ships stayed away from the war zone for fear of being attacked.
   b) American ships developed a prosperous shipping trade connecting colonies in the Caribbean with their French or Spanish homeland.
   c) Fierce competition sprang up between American, Dutch, and Swedish ships for the lucrative trade with France and Spain.
   d) Britain, France, and the United States agreed on a North Atlantic Free Trade Zone.
   e) The Royal Navy proclaimed a right to stop and seize American vessels engaged in trade that France and Spain had not allowed in peacetime.

8. The contributions of the United States navy to the War of 1812 included
   a) a daring raid on London, burning several Royal Navy ships and a row of docks.
   b) the victory of the *Constitution*, commanded by Isaac Hull, over the British frigate *Guerrière*.
   c) the stunning American victory over the British fleet at the Battle of Trafalgar.
   d) establishing control of Lakes Ontario and Erie, in the course of which Oliver Hazard Perry vanquished a British fleet in 1813.
   e) seizing the Virgin Islands and Cuba.

9. British strategy in 1814 launched invasions of the United States at
   a) New York by way of Lake Champlain and the Hudson River.
   b) the Southeast by an army from Florida and a naval attack on Charleston.
   c) Chicago and St. Louis via Lake Michigan and the Illinois River.

d) Washington, Baltimore, and Philadelphia from Chesapeake Bay.

e) New Orleans.

F. ESSAY QUESTIONS OR ORAL REPORTS

1. Look up the extent of actual Spanish and French control of the territory known as the Louisiana Purchase. What were the origins of the French claim to the territory? (Look at French exploration and trade from Canada as well as from New Orleans.) Where were French and Spanish settlements or fortifications located? What had been the history of contact, trade, and treaties with Native Americans in the territory? How much of the territory was simply unexplored, unknown, and effectively unclaimed by any European power or the United States?

2. Analyze the nation's reliance on an Electoral College to choose the president of the United States. How did this mechanism fail in 1800? Why had this weakness not become clear in the first three presidential elections? Compare the original theories favoring this method of election with current practice of presidential elections. What are the strengths and weaknesses of this method today, notably in the election of 2000? Can you devise a better method?

3. Analyze the long-term effect on American history of the Supreme Court's ruling in *Marbury* v. *Madison*. Was Justice Marshall's decision a wise and farsighted contribution to stable republican government, or a cynical manipulation of the law by a partisan politician? Did the decision take the country in a direction significantly different from that which Jefferson had hoped for it? When was the next time the Supreme Court exercised the power to nullify congressional legislation?

4. What were the economic and political relations between the United States and St. Domingue (after 1804 the Republic of Haiti)? Examine trade relations before and after the American Revolution, during the period of the French Revolution, and following the slave revolt in St. Domingue. After Toussaint L'Ouverture took command in St. Domingue, what were the diplomatic relations of his government with the Adams administration?

5. Analyze the tactics and strategy of the naval battles with the Barbary states of north Africa. Why did President Jefferson commit to these battles the tiny navy of the United States? How did the officers responsible succeed where more powerful European nations found it better policy to pay the tribute demanded?

6. Write a page or so making a case for declaring war on Great Britain in 1812 from the standpoint of a War Hawk. Then from the viewpoint of a New England merchant, whose ships routinely trade with the British West Indies, write a criticism of the decision to make war on Britain. Finally, write an overview of the reasons for disunity among Americans about the decision to go to war.

7. Assemble an account of Tecumseh's effort to unite Native American peoples in resistance to white settlement of the region west of the Appalachian Mountains. Include a brief biography of Tecumseh. Look up and report on how different tribes responded to his appeal, and why. Compare the religious revival led by his brother Tenskwatawa and the revival known as the Second Great Awakening, which was going on at the time among whites and to an extent African Americans.

The Seaboard and Inland Frontier

9

A. TERMS

Monroe Doctrine _____
_____
_____

necessary and proper _____
_____
_____

national treasury _____
_____
_____

paper money _____
_____
_____

specie reserve _____
_____
_____

Era of Good Feelings _____
_____
_____

universal suffrage _____
_____
_____

wildcat banks _____
_____
_____

hiring out _____
_____
_____

wage slavery _____
_____
_____

_____
_____

B. PHOTOGRAPHS

1. Select three characters at or around the table in this drawing. Write a speculative summary of what kind of person each was, in occupation, property owned, politics, and religious or moral convictions. Use documented information on actual lives and communities in the old West before 1830.

2. This painting has an imagined African landscape in the background, but may show a likeness of Cinqué's face. Write a one-page summary of the part of Africa he was actually taken from, his status and ethnic origin there, and what is known of his life after his return to Africa.

_____
_____
_____
_____
_____
_____
_____
_____
_____
_____
_____

_____
_____
_____
_____
_____
_____
_____
_____
_____
_____
_____
_____
_____
_____
_____
_____
_____
_____
_____
_____

3. Pick one of these individuals and assemble a two- or three-page biographical summary that includes information on how your individual spent the last ten years of life. Or write a comparison of the origins of each individual, what each became known for, and how each lived following the Civil War.

C. VOCABULARY

specie _____

_____

_____

currency _____

_____

bank note _____

_____

speculator _____

_____

cooper _____

_____

wheelwright _____

_____

artisan _____

_____

colonization _____

_____

abolitionism _____

_____

Freemason _____

_____

_____

D. INDIVIDUALS

Andrew Jackson _____

_____

John Quincy Adams _____

_____

James Monroe _____

_____

Nicholas Biddle _____

_____

_____

Horace King _____

_____

_____

Thomas Roderick Dew _____

_____

_____

Frederick Douglass _____

_____

_____

Denmark Vesey _____

_____

_____

Sojourner Truth _____

_____

_____

George Fitzhugh _____

_____

_____

Harriet Jacobs _____

_____

_____

John Randolph _____

_____

_____

Rufus King _____

_____

_____

Harrison Gray Otis _____

_____

_____

John C. Calhoun _____

_____

_____

James Tallmadge, Jr. _____

_____

_____

Sengbe Pieh (Cinqué) _____

_____

_____

Roger S. Baldwin _____

_____

_____

Martin Van Buren _____

_____

_____

E. MATCHING OR CIRCLE—circle the kinds of work common among slaves.

cook	blacksmith	butler	doctor	driver	wet nurse
lawyer	iron mill worker	jeweler	bank teller	nanny	cooper
secretary	miner	maid	overseer	weeder	harvester
ship captain	carpenter	teacher	architect	fieldhand	wheelwright

Place a number before each name on the left from the column at the right that designates the accomplishment or outlook of the person in column one.

___Eli Whitney
___Frederic Tudor
___Nathaniel Wyeth
___Simón Bolívar
___Daniel Webster
___David Walker
___Horace King
___Henry Clay
___William Wirt
___Dwight P. Janes

1. American System
2. rallied abolitionists to support *Amistad* mutineers
3. defended Dartmouth College charter
4. author of *Appeal* denouncing slavery
5. invented the ice cutter
6. eviction of Spain from Latin America
7. system of interchangeable parts
8. Anti-Mason candidate for president
9. civil engineer
10. shipped ice around the world

F. TRUE FALSE—circle one.

1. T F Frederic Tudor shipped cargoes of ice through two oceans, crossing the equator twice.
2. T F After the War of 1812, the Federalist Party recovered rapidly in power and national esteem.
3. T F After 1783 white males in every state had the right to vote and hold office.
4. T F Voting in the early nineteenth century was either by show of hands or by ballots taken unsealed from the voter's hand.
5. T F For a few years, New Jersey's constitution gave the vote to "all free inhabitants" of the state, which allowed a number of women to vote.
6. T F Spain was a world power with a wealthy colonial empire, posing a threat of a major military invasion in the event of a border dispute with the United States.
7. T F Many slaves crossed the border into Spanish Florida in search of freedom.
8. T F In the Transcontinental Treaty of 1819, Spain ceded Texas, New Mexico, Arizona, California, Nevada, and Utah to the United States.
9. T F New England supported protective tariffs for industry in 1816, while most congressional representatives from southern states opposed them.
10. T F The western and southern regions provided support for chartering the Second Bank of the United States.
11. T F In 1819 over five million acres of federal land were sold.

12. T F Under Nicholas Biddle, the Second Bank of the United States made secret payments to Daniel Webster and other politicians to protect it from hostile legislation.
13. T F The Supreme Court declared that the federal government could not interfere with New Hampshire's attempt to revoke the charter of Dartmouth College.
14. T F Visitors to the United States were especially offended by the common practice of spitting tobacco juice.
15. T F Soon after settlement in Mississippi and Alabama, social distinctions developed between planters who owned many slaves and farmers who had few slaves or none.
16. T F The inexhaustible fertility of New England's soil sustained a large population able to make the trek to settle lands in the West.
17. T F The upper Midwest was too rough and too much concerned with making money to be receptive to schooling and reform associations.
18. T F Many tobacco planters in Virginia and Maryland sold their depleted lands and moved to the southeastern states to resume a similar life.
19. T F Large planters settled on the richest lands in Alabama, Mississippi, Arkansas, and Louisiana, pushing poorer settlers into the backlands.
20. T F In planning a slave revolt in 1800 in Virginia, Gabriel particularly singled out Quakers and Methodists to be exterminated during the uprising.
21. T F In 1831 and 1832 the legislature of Virginia debated emancipation of slaves in the state.
22. T F The abolitionist movement began in New England in the 1830s.
23. T F The upper classes of both races in New Orleans shared a French cultural heritage.
24. T F In 1860 half a million African Americans were free, half in the North, half in the South.
25. T F President John Quincy Adams wanted to lessen federal involvement in science and economic development.
26. T F The *Amistad* case turned on whether the captives had been captured in Africa, which was considered piracy, or born in the Americas, in which case they were legally slaves.
27. T F Partly because black republics might have raised the issue of slavery, Congress delayed support for sending a delegation to a meeting of American nations in Panama.
28. T F Since western Protestant Scots-Irish settlers supported Andrew Jackson for president, Roman Catholic Irish immigrants opposed him.
29. T F Children of slaves did no work until they were ten or twelve years old.
30. T F Slaves on the sugar plantations of Louisiana operated complicated machinery for refining sugarcane juice and for manufacturing molasses and crystal sugar.

H. MULTIPLE CHOICE—circle one or more correct answers.
1. Frederic Tudor's ice exporting business
   a) was enriched by high prices during the 1807 embargo and the War of 1812.
   b) shipped twelve thousand tons in 1836, and 146,000 by 1856, to ports all over the world.
   c) charged high prices even to new customers, because there was no competition.
   d) drew an angry outcry from preservationists for disturbing the natural cycle of New England ponds.
   e) began with a purchase of ice for Martinique.

2. The Monroe Doctrine, delivered in the president's annual message to Congress in 1823,
   a) made a strong impression on foreign countries acknowledging the power of the United States.
   b) grew out of communication from Britain urging that the two countries join in recognizing the independence of new Latin American republics.
   c) suggested it would be appropriate in the future for European nations to seek colonies in Africa rather than in America.
   d) committed the United States to a policy framed by John Quincy Adams, who served as Monroe's secretary of state.
   e) invited Mexico to seek admission to the United States, which would protect the proprietors of large estates from rebellion by their Indian peasant workforce.

3. The Second Bank of the United States, chartered in 1816 for a period of twenty years,
   a) received an annual subsidy from the federal government.
   b) established its headquarters in Washington, D.C., with a branch in Philadelphia.
   c) had twenty-five directors, five chosen by the president with the approval of the Senate, the rest chosen by private stockholders.
   d) received payments to the government and handled government payments, including salaries of federal employees.
   e) was prohibited from making private loans or issuing paper money.

4. The enslaved people who took over the *Amistad*
   a) planned to start a rebellion of slaves throughout the Americas.
   b) seized the ship shortly after departure from Africa, intending to sail to Haiti.
   c) had been unloaded illegally to the *Amistad* by a Portuguese ship off the coast of Havana with false papers showing they were already residents of Cuba.
   d) were intercepted by a ship of the United States navy commanded by abolitionist officers.
   e) returned to Africa after a federal court and the Supreme Court found that they had been illegally taken into slavery.

5. During the presidential campaign of 1828, it was charged that
   a) John Quincy Adams had pimped for Czar Alexander I when he was minister to Russia.
   b) Andrew Jackson was a brute for ordering the execution of six militamen during the Creek War in 1813.
   c) John Quincy Adams had a personal billiard table in the Executive Mansion and wore silk underwear.
   d) Andrew Jackson and his wife Rachel had "lived in sin" before their marriage.
   e) John Quincy Adams had won the presidency in 1824 by a "corrupt bargain" that cheated Jackson of his victory in the popular vote.

6. To secure cooperation among slaves, their owners offered
   a) cash prizes of several thousand dollars for the most productive harvest hands.
   b) free time to cultivate private gardens, and use of land to grow the garden.
   c) vacations and freedom to travel after ten years of faithful service.
   d) approval to visit friends on neighboring plantations, and to take a spouse.
   e) customary holidays such as Christmas, with the giving of small gifts.

7. Which of these statements would describe the conditions of family life for people held as slaves during the nineteenth century?
   a) Slave codes in state laws offered specific protection to the sanctity of the family.
   b) Shrewd masters seeking stability on the plantation encouraged marriage and fidelity among their slaves.
   c) Slaveowners had the opportunity to commit rape on any slave they held, and resistance on the part of the victim or her husband could bring retaliation.
   d) Mothers had more authority than fathers in slave households, because they did more important work on the plantation and sold for a higher price.
   e) In about two of three slave families, both mother and father raised the children.

8. Studies of wealth and income in the United States in 1840 show that
   a) the new cotton-growing states west of the Appalachians drew an annual income well above the national average.
   b) northeastern states, enriched by heavy industrial development, accumulated twice as much wealth as the southern agricultural states.
   c) southern Atlantic coastal states had a lower annual income than northeastern states.
   d) states formed from the Northwest Territory were the poorest section of the United States.
   e) property values on southern plantations were low and generated resentment among their owners at being poorer than wealthy classes in other regions.

9 The Tallmadge Amendment, which split Congress along sectional lines, provided that
   a) all slaves in Missouri territory must be freed before it could be admitted as a state.
   b) Missouri should be admitted to the Union as a slave state without conditions
   c) Missouri should be admitted as a slave state and Maine as a free state.
   d) all children born to slaves in Missouri would be free after reaching the age of twenty-five.
   e) no slaves not already belonging to people living there could be introduced into the state.

ESSAY QUESTIONS OR ORAL REPORTS

1. Catalog the requirements for voting in three states in 1800 versus 1830. Examine variations within regions, such as New England, the South, and the Northwest Territory. Were there general patterns that differed from region to region?

2. Examine Mexico's revolution against Spain in the early nineteenth century. What classes or interests engaged in the revolution, and which classes opposed it? Did the Indian peasant and worker population on the whole side with revolutionaries in the white upper classes? Were there differences in objectives even among interests that were on the same side?

3. Study the preparation and course of Gabriel's rebellion in Virginia in 1800, Denmark Vesey's in South Carolina in 1822, or Nat Turner's in Virginia in 1831. What kinds of work had the rebellious slaves been accustomed to doing? Did the revolts you chose have a serious chance of succeeding? Define what would have constituted success.

4. Examine the evolution of slavery in Virginia in the early nineteenth century. How different from the economic foundations of the slave system of Virginia in the eighteenth century were its foundations in the nineteenth? Examine changes in state laws in the 1820s and 1830s. Why did the southern view of slavery as a regrettable but temporarily necessary evil give way among some Virginians to a view of it as a positive good?

_____
_____
_____
_____
_____
_____
_____
_____
_____
_____
_____
_____
_____
_____
_____
_____
_____
_____
_____

A Nation at Work: Labor, Transportation, and the Economy

10

A. TERMS

transportation revolution _____
_____
_____

community markets _____
_____
_____

navigable river _____
_____
_____

screw propeller _____
_____
_____

canal locks _____
_____
_____

packet boats _____
_____
_____

waterpower _____
_____
_____

steam engine _____
_____
_____

interchangeable parts _____
_____
_____

national roads _____

_____

domestic system _____

_____

Bessemer process _____

_____

labor union _____

_____

limited liability _____

_____

domestic servant _____

_____

balloon frame house _____

_____

clipper ship _____

_____

scrimshaw _____

_____

utopian socialism _____

_____

cooperative communities _____

_____

B. PHOTOGRAPHS

1. Explain how the locks made it possible for boats to go over the Appalachian barrier from Lake Erie to Albany, New York; detail their method of operation. Also identify the natural waterways that were part of the Erie Canal system. How long was the Erie Canal commercially useful, and why did it go out of use? What happened to the economy of the communities that had grown up to serve traffic on the canal?

_____

_____

_____

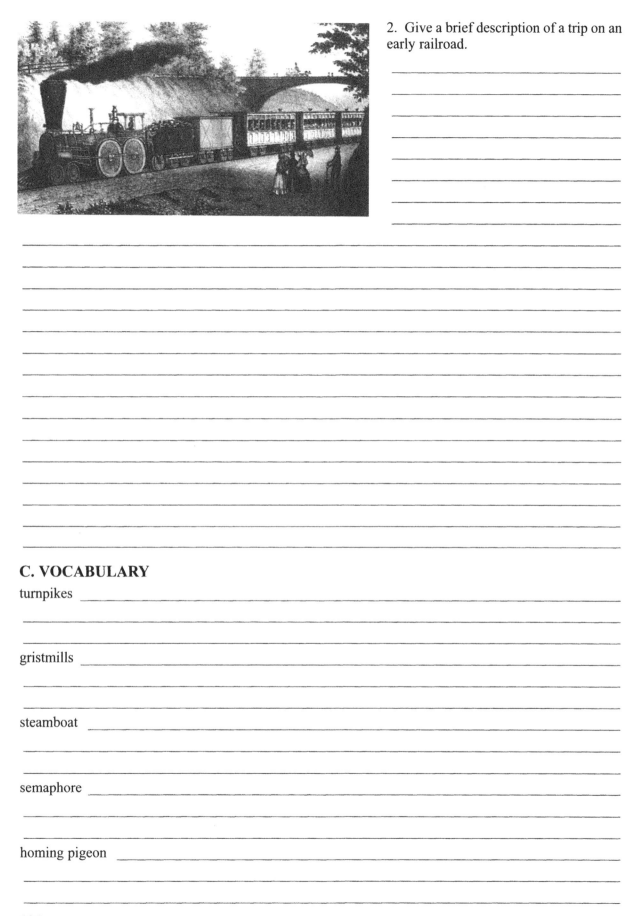

2. Give a brief description of a trip on an early railroad.

_____

_____

_____

_____

_____

_____

_____

_____

_____

_____

_____

_____

_____

_____

_____

_____

_____

_____

_____

_____

_____

_____

_____

_____

C. VOCABULARY

turnpikes _____

_____

gristmills _____

_____

steamboat _____

_____

semaphore _____

_____

homing pigeon _____

_____

_____

spinning jenny _____

_____

engineer _____

_____

magnate _____

_____

mechanization _____

_____

Flying Cloud _____

_____

proprietorship _____

_____

partnership _____

_____

corporation _____

_____

incorporation _____

_____

blacksmith _____

_____

cast-steel plow _____

_____

phalanx _____

_____

spermaceti _____

_____

ambergris _____

_____

cobbler _____

_____

tanner _____

_____

workers' strike _____

_____

D. INDIVIDUALS

Samuel F.B. Morse _____

_____

DeWitt Clinton _____

_____

Charles Dickens _____

_____

Robert Fulton _____

_____

Samuel Slater _____

_____

Smith Brown _____

_____

Francis Cabot Lowell _____

_____

John Deere _____

_____

Oliver Evans _____

_____

Samuel Colt _____
_____
_____

Elias Howe _____
_____
_____

Charles Fourier _____
_____
_____

Cyrus McCormick _____
_____
_____

Isaac Singer _____
_____
_____

Isaac Guggenheim _____
_____
_____

E. MATCH OR CIRCLE—circle which of these new technologies or items of machinery were invented in the United States.

Franklin stove	Bessemer steel process	steel-bladed plow
steel rails for railroads	interchangeable parts	spinning jenny
cotton gin	telegraph	automatic weaving machinery
railroad locomotives	mechanical mule	fully workable steamboat

F. TRUE FALSE—circle one.

1. T F Between 1815 and the Civil War, the coordinated national economy that had emerged after the Revolution diversified into disconnected regional and local economies.
2. T F By 1820 privately owned turnpikes were some of the best roads in the United States.
3. T F The census of 1820 indicates a significant number of steamboats plying the Great Lakes.
4. T F The steamboat *Helen McGregor* exploded while leaving the dock in Memphis, throwing passengers in the river where many were killed by the boiling water or by inhaling live steam.
5. T F By 1815 New York City was well established as the nation's largest port, far ahead of Boston, Philadelphia, Baltimore, and Charleston combined.
6. T F Private enterprise would have built the Erie Canal, but Governor DeWitt Clinton of New York insisted on getting the state directly involved.
7. T F Between 1817 and 1830, the cost to ship freight from Buffalo to New York City dropped significantly.
8. T F The first railways in Britain were horse-drawn carts on rails, hauling coal from the mines to ships for transport.
9. T F Much of the labor in early New England spinning mills was done by children between the ages of seven and thirteen.
10. T F The Lowell mills in Massachusetts were an early focus of criticism by social reformers, and served as a model for some of Charles Dickens's dreariest novels.

11. T F An early patent of the United States was for a process of hauling grain to the top of a four-story mill, then using gravity to move the grain through drying, spreading, and grinding.
12. T F The census of 1850 counted 1.2 million Americans.
13. T F Prior to 1840, most Americans bought their clothes from England, France, and Holland.
14. T F Until the early 1840s, the United States imported most of its iron from Europe.
15. T F American iron production was handled by large enterprises that amounted to industrial plantations, owning large stretches of land and housing workers on company property.
16. T F Henry Bessemer developed a method for making cheap steel that immediately put the American steel industry well ahead of its kind in Europe.
17. T F Limited liability stock companies made each investor personally responsible for the success or failure of the company and all its debts.
18. T F Over half of working Americans in 1850 were engaged in agriculture.
19. T F In 1850 ten million American construction workers were employed building roads, homes, streets, churches, and factories.
20. T F By the time of the Civil War, the Irish name "Bridget" was associated with servant girls.
21. T F Clergymen and school teachers were among the best paid of the educated classes between 1820 and 1860.
22. T F Working hours in American industries before the Civil War were ten to thirteen hours a day, usually for six days every week, without any vacations.
23. T F The option of moving west and acquiring cheap land contributed to the failure of Utopian socialist industrial communities.
24. T F After the Panic of 1837, thousands of workers lost jobs, employers cut wages, and the union movement in the United States collapsed.
25. T F Employers welcomed pragmatic trade unions as an acceptable alternative to Utopian socialist and other radical movements.
26. T F By 1840, industry had replaced agriculture as the chief occupation of Americans, and the largest source of income for the nation as a whole.
27. T F In the "hungry forties" impoverished European immigrants desperate for work began to pour into the United States, competing with native-born Americans for mill jobs.
28. T F Harvest hands in the Midwest in the 1850s were poorly paid, because there were so many migrants seeking each available job.

G. MULTIPLE CHOICE—circle one or more correct answers.

1. Charles Dickens's trip to the United States in 1842 provoked several responses and observations, including these:
   a) Mobs of slave owners attempted to lynch him as a dangerous radical.
   b) He was criticized as selfish and mercenary when he complained that American publishers were failing to pay royalties for printing and selling his books.
   c) He was cheered and royally entertained at balls and banquets in Boston.
   d) He expressed admiration for the scenery, people, and railroad accommodations.
   e) He was favorably impressed with the workers and facilities in Lowell, Massachusetts factories.

2. The best known features of Mississippi and Ohio steamboat traffic included
   a) a shallow craft to float on low water levels over shifting sandbars.
   b) massive coal-burning engines requiring coal chutes at major ports.
   c) a lack of storage or cabins below, so that passengers and freight were piled up on deck.
   d) dangerous accidents from snags in the river bottom and boiler explosions.
   e) an enormous reduction in the time of upstream travel and downstream freight rates.

3. Canals built across the country, in awareness of how profitable the Erie Canal was, included
   a) the Main Line system from Philadelphia, requiring 174 locks, a financial failure.
   b) the Minnehaha Canal connecting Lake Superior to St. Paul, Minnesota.
   c) canals connecting the Ohio River to Lake Erie via three different river systems.
   d) the Peachtree Canal connecting the Tennessee River to the Savannah River.
   e) the Chesapeake and Ohio Canal, built from Alexandria, Virginia, and Washington, D.C.

4. These were true of Samuel Slater's textile mills:
   a) They employed a thousand workers and up, drawn from farms into medium and large cities.
   b) Mill families lived in houses provided by the employer, who also required them to attend church and shop in stores owned by mill operators.
   c) Wages were typically in chits for use at the local store.
   d) Mill owners faced hostility from the local community if they hired children.
   e) Families were allowed a piece of land to grow vegetables, and for a fee could graze cows or horses on company-owned pasture land.

5. The development of interchangeable parts in industry
   a) was a closely kept secret of British industry, gradually exported to the United States.
   b) was proposed by Eli Whitney in 1798 for production of firearms.
   c) raised the price of an ordinary alarm clock to $15.00.
   d) was fully feasible only after Simeon North invented the first drilling machine.
   e) lowered the price of many manufactured goods so more people could afford them.

6. These statements are true of American clothing in the first half of the nineteenth-century United States:
   a) Until the generation preceding the Civil War, Americans wore clothes produced in their own homes.
   b) Factories began manufacturing coarse industrial grade cloth that became the standard for workers and poor families generally, lowering comfort, quality, and durability.
   c) Homemade clothing was costly; few people wore underwear, and children in summer often wore nothing but a long shirt.
   d) Sewing machines made it so much easier to make clothes at home that there was no real market for commercially produced clothing.
   e) Factories were developed that produced large amounts of clothing for sale by retailers, soon accepted by workers and the middle class.

7. Merchants, wholesalers, and retailers, who made their living buying and selling other people's commodities,
   a) all together amounted to more than half a million people in the United States around 1850.
   b) served no useful function, simply buying low and selling high for a profit.
   c) excluded immigrants and non-Christians from doing business, by use of exclusive trade agreements among native-born Protestants.
   d) included rich merchants in port cities, wholesalers of inland cities, small retail merchants, and thousands of peddlers.
   e) were in some cases producers as well, selling their own products.

8. Matched against wages for similar work in Europe, American wages in the 1820s were
   a) extremely low, making life a great disappointment for new immigrants.
   b) about the same, but the desire for political freedom motivated immigration.
   c) about thirty percent higher than in Britain, and even better compared with wages in other countries.
   d) much better for skilled craft workers, but much worse for unskilled workers.
   e) an important motivation for millions of immigrants from Europe.

9. Work in early American industry could be accurately described as
   a) healthier than it is today, because there was plenty of fresh air, well-balanced exercise, and less exposure to infectious disease.
   b) performed in searing heat and biting cold with little protection and much exposure to polluted air.
   c) bringing many risks of injury or death on the job from cave-ins and unprotected machinery.
   d) enjoying a wide-open job market, with so many options that employers had to provide extra benefits to attract workers.
   e) involving frequent exposure to dangerous chemicals that sickened workers over time.

10. Trade unions had developed in the United States by 1815 to the point that
   a) employers feared and detested unions for denying them power over their workers and interfering with the setting of pay rates by free market forces alone.
   b) Congress held extensive debates on whether the power to regulate interstate commerce included the power to pass federal laws against unions.
   c) during prosperous times when the labor market was tight, unions could secure shorter workdays and higher hourly pay.
   d) slaves in several states attempted to form unions as a means of improving their own working conditions and benefits of employment.
   e) unions began to be a major force in relations between labor and capital, with the outlines of a system of national unions—until the Panic of 1837.

11. Agriculture in the United States changed from 1820 to 1850 in these ways.
   a) As industry grew, people in New England lost interest in raising crops.
   b) New states north of the Ohio River produced wheat and corn more cheaply than the eastern states, which could not compete.
   c) Cotton became the dominant crop in states that had the right climate to grow it.
   d) Soil became depleted, and food imported from South America was cheaper to buy.
   e) Farmers in New England, New York, Pennsylvania, and New Jersey turned to growing fruits and vegetables for sale in nearby cities.

H. ESSAY QUESTIONS OR ORAL REPORTS

1. For the first half of the nineteenth century consider the role of improved transportation in defining the United States as a nation. What were the realistic expectations of the most ardent nationalists, prior to 1815, for welding together a single unified nation from the individual states?

2. Assemble an overview of the effect of interchangeable parts on American industries. Identify some of the first industries to apply it. Why did this process make production more efficient? How did it prolong the useful life of machinery? Why were interchangeable parts employed first to manufacture guns?

3. Consider the character and effect of the innovation in corporate structure in the early nineteenth century. What does limited liability mean? How did the rise of corporations change the market economy of the nation and take the place of the agrarian vision of Thomas Jefferson?

4. Write a review of agricultural markets in 1850. Consider what market a farmer could sell to. Look for such information as what corn was selling for in Illinois as opposed to what it sold for in New York. What were the transportation costs for corn or other commodities? Productivity of soil and whether the local climate is right for a certain crop need some consideration as well.

5. Prepare a demographic analysis of the American whaling industry. Where did ship crews come from? Where did officers and captains come from? What industries depended on whale products? What household comforts depended on the whale trade?

6. Analyze the development of the textile industry in New England. Which parts of the New England industry were linked to the cotton economy? What contrasting patterns of employment, if any, did different textile companies try? How did the industry change the character and politics of New England during the first half of the century?

Perfectionism, 1800–1850   11

A. TERMS

Second Great Awakening _____
_____
_____

perfectionism _____
_____
_____

republican institutions _____
_____
_____

camp meetings _____
_____
_____

Burned Over District _____
_____
_____

separation of church and state _____
_____
_____

infant baptism _____
_____
_____

sabbatarianism _____
_____
_____

Church of Jesus Christ of Latter-Day Saints _____
_____
_____

transcendentalism _____
_____
_____

redemption _____

_____

colonization of freed slaves _____

_____

abolitionism _____

_____

B. PHOTOGRAPHS

1. Identify and describe at least five events of daily life portrayed in this picture, such as water being obtained from a public pump at lower left. What do these tell you about the general pattern of life, technology, and means of survival in the era preceding the Civil War?

Write a paragraph comparing the total image in this painting to the reputation and actual condition of late twentieth-century American slums.

_____

_____

_____

_____

_____

_____

_____

_____
_____
_____
_____
_____
_____
_____
_____
_____
_____
_____
_____
_____
_____
_____
_____

2. Write one page comparing the presentation of alcoholism in this nineteenth-century caricature with modern-day approaches toward alcohol consumption, or toward use of other intoxicating or mind-altering drugs.

The MORNING DRAM.

The Beginning of Sorrow, Neglect of Business, Idleness, Languor, Loss of Appetite, Dulness and Heaviness, a love of Strong Drink increasing.

The GROG SHOP.

Bad Company, Profaneness, Cursing and Swearing, Quarreling & Fighting, Gambling, Obscenity, Ridicule and Hatred of Religion. The Gate of Hell.

The CONFIRMED DRUNKARD.

Beastly Intoxication, Loss of Character, Loss of Natural Affection, Family Suffering, Brutality, Misery, Disease, Mortgages, Sheriffs, Writs &c.

CONCLUDING SCENE.

Poverty, Wretchedness, a Curse and Burden upon Society, Want, Beggary, Pauperism, Death.

_____
_____
_____
_____
_____
_____
_____
_____

_____

_____

_____

_____

_____

_____

_____

_____

_____

_____

_____

_____

_____

_____

_____

_____

_____

_____

_____

_____

_____

_____

C. VOCABULARY

utilitarian _____

_____

Unitarianism _____

_____

freethinkers _____

_____

revival _____

_____

church circuits _____

_____

Adventism _____

_____

Millennialist _____
_____
_____

spiritualism _____
_____
_____

temperance _____
_____
_____

Sabbatarian _____
_____
_____

humanitarian _____
_____
_____

penitentiary _____
_____
_____

asylum _____
_____
_____

D. INDIVIDUALS

Mother Ann Lee _____
_____

Lyman Beecher _____
_____

Charles Grandison Finney _____
_____

William Miller _____
_____

Joseph Smith _____
_____
_____

Katie and Maggie Fox _____

_____

John Humphrey Noyes _____

_____

William Ellery Channing _____

_____

Lewis Tappan _____

_____

Alexis de Tocqueville _____

_____

Dorothea Dix _____

_____

Samuel Gridley Howe _____

_____

William Lloyd Garrison _____

_____

Theodore Weld _____

_____

Neal Dow _____

_____

Angelina and Sarah Grimké _____

_____

Charles Fourier _____

_____

Elijah Lovejoy _____

_____

_____

John Quincy Adams _____

_____

_____

James G. Birney _____

_____

_____

Elizabeth Cady Stanton _____

_____

_____

Herman Melville _____

_____

_____

Horace Mann _____

_____

_____

Wendell Phillips _____

_____

_____

Ralph Waldo Emerson _____

_____

_____

Henry David Thoreau _____

_____

_____

Susan B. Anthony _____

_____

_____

Mary Lyon _____

_____

_____

Nathaniel Hawthorne _____

_____

_____

Lucretia Mott _____

_____

_____

Edgar Allan Poe _____

_____

_____

Benjamin Lundy _____

_____

_____

Margaret Fuller _____

_____

_____

E. MATCHING—Place corresponding letter to left of number.

___ 1. Rejected all, or almost all, the precepts of organized religion.

___ 2. Marked by dignified and elaborate ritual and ceremony; attracted the upper classes in both North and South.

___ 3. Influential among well-educated New Englanders, who rejected what they considered irrational in traditional Christianity.

___ 4. Centered church life in the independent communities of worship and in its earlier days had emphasized the inherent sinfulness of man and salvation for an elect.

___ 5. Despite much in common with Congregationalism theologically, this group had a hierarchal structure of church government.

___ 6. Believed that biblical revelation had been supplemented by the Book of Morman.

___ 7. Believed in salvation for sinners who sincerely and freely repent and submit to God's will.

___ 8. Believed the Bible alone guides true Christians, who have the right and duty to interpret the book for themselves.

___ 9. Combined the passion of a conversion experience with a life of labor and charity in service to God.

___10. Expected the Second Coming of Christ in the near future, initially projecting a series of dates in the 1840s.

___11. Communicated with the dead or obtained messages from the spirit world through a medium.

A. Congregationalist

B. freethinkers

C. Methodism

D. Episcopal (Anglican)

E. Disciples of Christ

F. Presbyterian

G. spiritualism

H. Unitarianism

I. Church of Jesus Christ of Latter-Day Saints

J. Adventists

K. Baptists and Methodists

F. TRUE FALSE—circle one.

1. T F   In the era before the Civil War, at least ten percent of young urban women in the United States turned to prostitution at least part of their lives.

2. T F   Employers in the first half of the nineteenth century often paid carpenters, printers, and ship-wrights part of their wages in beer, wine, or whiskey.

3. T F   Shaker belief in humility and simplicity led them to produce crude, ugly furniture that was uncomfortable to use and easily fell apart.

4. T F   The preacher Peter Cartwright described Sunday in Logan County, Kentucky, as a day set apart for hunting, fishing, horse-racing, card-playing, and dancing.

5. T F   Between 1800 and 1820, church attendance in the United States increased rapidly, especially in the newly settled regions west of the Appalachian Mountains.

6. T F   The Second Great Awakening brought new members to the Shakers, who taught that God possesses both male and female attributes and that sexual intercourse is the basis of all evil.

7. T F Joseph Smith announced plans to run for president of the United States on a platform of freeing all prisoners, emancipating all slaves, and annexing California, Oregon, Mexico, and Canada.
8. T F Revivalism created grave doubts among its practitioners, implanted questions concerning faith, and produced a rationalist form of religion.
9. T F After his Christian conversion experience, John Humphrey Noyes founded the Oneida community, basing it on "communism of property" and communal marriage.
10. T F In 1820 whiskey cost less than tea or coffee.
11. T F Roman Catholic immigrants demanded strict enforcement of Sabbath laws that would shut down sports events, close taverns, and forbid businesses from opening on Sundays.
12. T F Sunday schools regularly taught temperance lessons in the 1840s, but public schools were prohibited by law from advocating that children refrain from drinking alcohol.
13. T F In most states until around 1840, failure to pay debts was a criminal offense that could lead to indefinite jail sentences.
14. T F Dorothea Dix was so immersed in her work on behalf of the mentally ill that she urged nurses not to leave work in hospitals to serve the sick and wounded in the Civil War.
15. T F Penitentiaries were originally so named because they were designed to make "penitents" of their inmates—to bring about a moral rehabilitation, not just to punish.
16. T F Slavery had seldom existed anywhere in the world before it was instituted in the Americas as a result of the transatlantic trade from Africa.
17. T F The Virginia legislature's last serious debate about abolishing slavery in the state was in 1832 following Nat Turner's rebellion.
18. T F Many states that abolished slavery before the Civil War also had laws restricting the civil rights of free African American residents and barring others from entering the state.
19. T F By 1830 there were hardly any free African Americans in the United States, and none at all in any southern state.
20. T F Amos Kendall, postmaster general under President Andrew Jackson, illegally allowed postmasters to confiscate abolitionist literature from the mails.
21. T F When Abby Kelley was chosen for an executive post of the American Anti-Slavery Society, many members who opposed such a role for women were alienated from the organization.

G. MULTIPLE CHOICE—circle one or more correct answers.

1. A famous camp meeting in 1801 at Cane Ridge, Kentucky,
    a) attracted twenty thousand people for six days of feverish exhortation.
    b) marked the end of the Second Great Awakening and a turning away from religion.
    c) was conducted in a calm and orderly manner, without convulsion or fainting.
    d) featured the impassioned preaching of eighteen Presbyterian, one African-American Baptist, and four Methodist ministers.
    e) was an isolated frontier event.

2. Mormons generated hostility at one time or another because
    a) as a tightly knit group they threatened to become a powerful voting bloc.
    b) they were opposed to slavery and too friendly to Indians.
    c) migration to the Great Salt Lake basin triggered fears of war with Mexico.
    d) Irish immigrants resented Mormon recruitment in British factory towns.
    e) some Mormons practiced polygamous marriage.

3. The Five Points district of New York City in the 1830s and 1840s
    a) featured some of the most prominent mansions in the country.
    b) was notorious for its brothels employing ten thousand women.
    c) contained the city's financial centers when Wall Street was mostly residential.
    d) had become crowded with tenements as miserable as any in Europe.
    e) was still a quiet middle-class neighborhood of no special note.

4. Instances of mob violence in New York during the 1830s and 1840s were
    a) heated rallies demonstrating widespread opposition to annexation of Texas and war with Mexico.
    b) municipal election rivalries between Whigs and Democrats, which touched off three days of rioting in 1834.
    c) riots between working-class fans of the actor Edwin Forrest and upper-class admirers of William Charles Macready.
    d) anti-abolitionist fury, which at one point burned an African Methodist Episcopal Church.
    e) annual battles with clubs and knives by bands from each of the five boroughs.

5. The effort to improve the policing of American cities brought
    a) bitter debate between the Democratic Party, which advocated a strong local police presence, and the Whig Party, which believed that only the federal government could establish such a police force.
    b) abandonment of the colonial system of part-time constables and night watchmen, who were untrained and often ran from disturbances instead of stopping them.
    c) vigorous recruitment efforts in Ireland to secure men believed to be pious but strong, and free of local loyalties that might impair objective enforcement.
    d) temptation of payoffs to the newly uniformed police officers for allowing illegal activities to continue.
    e) hiring of uniformed police in New York in the 1840s, Philadelphia in 1850, Boston in 1854, and Baltimore in 1857.

6. The General Union for Promoting the Observance of the Christian Sabbath
    a) was formed in 1828 in Rochester, New York, and led by Lyman Beecher and Lewis Tappan.
    b) deluged Congress with petitions that Sunday delivery of United States mail be stopped.
    c) organized mobs to throw rocks at anyone driving a cart on Sunday, and to break the windows of any business open for Sunday shoppers.
    d) urged the president to pack the Supreme Court with justices who would favor laws closing down businesses on Sunday.
    e) opened a Sabbatarian stage coach company so that Christians would not have to patronize businesses that broke the Sabbath.

7. The Auburn Penitentiary built by New York State following the War of 1812
    a) had narrow and poorly ventilated cells that made many inmates sick and drove some insane.
    b) was entrusted to a staff of Quakers who treated each inmate well and developed classes providing spiritual and vocational instruction.
    c) after 1823 confined prisoners to their cells only at night; during the day they worked in prison workshops.
    d) kept political prisoners in specially designed dungeons below the water table, where rats competed for the rotting food served as meals.
    e) to the state's benefit kept masses of prisoners under control without need of a large supervisory force and produced goods the state sold for a profit.

8. Pennsylvania's Eastern State Penitentiary at Cherry Hill, built in 1829,
    a) resembled a series of Quaker meeting houses separated by small dormitories.
    b) resembled a medieval fortress with a high stone wall and an octagonal guard tower.
    c) had a poor sanitation system even for the early nineteenth century, supplying drinking water in the same buckets used as toilets the rest of the day.
    d) allowed inmates visits only from chaplains, prison officials, and officers of approved charitable organizations, forbidding visits from family or friends.
    e) proved to be expensive to run, and the severe isolation of prisoners produced emotional breakdown.

9. Social influences in the Unites States that produced a movement to abolish slavery included
    a) enlightenment philosophies that centered human personality on freely exercised reason, a capacity that makes slavery a violation of the human character of the slave.
    b) a growing recognition of the moral superiority of medieval African kingdoms.

c) discomfort even among slaveholders for a time after the American Revolution, which made popular a language of freedom and liberty.

d) evangelical Christianity, which defined all human beings as equally children of sin and equally called to redemption.

e) military service by Americans of all regions and colors in the Mexican War.

10. The proposal that freed slaves be colonized in Africa or elsewhere
   a) won support from leading non-African politicians, including Thomas Jefferson, Henry Clay, James Madison, and Abraham Lincoln.
   b) was pressed by the American Colonization Society, which planted in Liberia on the west African coast a settlement of black Americans.
   c) drew funding from Cornelius Vanderbilt and John Jacob Astor to pay transportation costs for the thousands of people to be colonized.
   d) brought an offer by diplomatic emissaries from the Songhay Empire and the Asante Union to receive freed slaves and provide them with their own land to farm.
   e) was of little interest to African Americans, who insisted that the United States belonged to them as much as any white residents.

11. The establishment of a seminary at Oberlin College, the result of division in evangelical Christian ranks, was related to these incidents:
   a) A younger group of theology students denied the authority of Scripture and began rewriting the four gospels.
   b) Disciples of the evangelist Charles Finney helped convert to the abolitionist cause students at Lane Theological Seminary in Cincinnati.
   c) Missionaries from the Oneida Colony in New York clashed with the rigorous morality of most Christians in Ohio.
   d) The administration at Lane headed by Lyman Beecher had set itself against students who advocated immediate abolition and social equality for free African Americans.
   e) Finney helped abolitionists, led by Theodore Weld, to obtain from the wealthy merchants Lewis and Arthur Tappan financial backing for the establishment of the Oberlin seminary.

H. ESSAY QUESTIONS OR ORAL REPORTS

1. Taking any one western state or territory in the first half of the nineteenth century, identify what social classes moved there, and from what eastern states and foreign countries the migrants came. What in the new settlements made religious devotion difficult or to the contrary encouraged it? Briefly summarize some of the primary missionary efforts and the results they achieved.

2. Select a denomination that either formed during the Second Great Awakening, or had become prominent in the colonies during the first Great Awakening and continued to be influential in the second. Trace the origins and growth of this denomination. Demonstrate factual knowledge of the denomination's origin and development.

3. Analyze the responses to American religion and culture on the part of a religious faith, such as the Jewish, Roman Catholic, or Islamic religion, that planted itself in the United States largely through immigration rather than revival. How did immigrants relate to the American social and political system they found themselves in? How did religious authorities within the faith you are examining respond to the form of religious freedom defined in the United States? Is there any indication that later leaders of the faith took a position toward the nation's cultural and religious diversity that differed from the ways the leaders had looked on the country in the early immigrant days?

4. Develop an overview of crime and law enforcement in any two cities between 1830 and 1860. Obtain what is available in the way of crime statistics from the whole three decades. What kind of law enforcement was available during that period? How well did it cope? What changes in police presence and practice were introduced during this period?

5. Look up and summarize when, where, and how the interstate sale of slaves became an established and profitable business. What regions were primarily sources of slaves for resale, and where were they mostly sold to? What effect did the slave trade have on family life, religious practice, and education among slaves?

6. Write an overview of abolitionist movements in the southern states from 1800 to 1830. Include the work of Benjamin Lundy in Baltimore, Samuel Doak and Elihu Embree in Tennessee, and James G. Birney in Alabama. Then show when, why, and how antislavery activity was eliminated from any effective presence in slave states.

7. Look up records of Dorothea Dix's original presentations to a state legislature. Evaluate what in that state improved in the lives of the patients she spoke for. What were the continuing flaws in the new institutions and treatment?

8. William Lloyd Garrison believed that an accurate portrayal of slavery and its evils would rouse the public in support of abolitionism. But for many years, uncompromising advocates of abolishing slavery encountered hostility and violent reprisals in the North. For any one northern state, explore the reasons why so many people there were hostile to abolitionists. Be sure to examine how different classes responded. Did people feel threatened by abolition? Why? Did the cause of ending slavery suffer from resentments against the perceived arrogance of reformers generally: for instance, advocates of temperance?

An Empire for Slavery   12

A. TERMS

Jacksonian democracy _____

_____

_____

common man _____

_____

_____

Second Party System _____

_____

_____

spoils of office _____

_____

_____

internal improvements _____

_____

_____

states' rights _____

_____

_____

federal supremacy _____

_____

_____

the Bank War _____

_____

_____

Remember the Alamo! _____

_____

_____

credit reserves _____

_____

_____

Specie Circular _____

_____

manifest destiny _____

_____

Santa Fe Trail _____

_____

wagon train _____

_____

joint occupation _____

_____

B. PHOTOGRAPHS

1. Would you have voted for any of these men for president of the United States? Explain why or why not.

2. Write an alternate scenario to the Trail of Tears. What would have been necessary for the Cherokee to remain in their original homeland? How would the subsequent history of the United States have differed?

_____

_____

_____

_____

_____

_____

_____

_____

_____

_____

_____

_____

_____

_____

_____

_____

_____

_____

_____

_____

_____

_____

3. Consider a soldier marching the Cherokee west, a Cherokee mother trying to get her children safely through the journey, a Cherokee man having to deal with the soldiers and the trail, and an army contractor supplying the trip. Write a paragraph summarizing what each might have been thinking.

C. VOCABULARY

caucus

Whigs

protective tariff

nullification _____
_____

monopoly _____
_____

panic (economic) _____
_____

entrepreneur _____
_____

bonds _____
_____

log cabin _____
_____

laissez-faire _____
_____

bullion _____
_____

tallow _____
_____

hard cider _____
_____

ranchero _____
_____

Californio _____
_____

annexation _____
_____

D. INDIVIDUALS

John Tyler _____

_____

Marcus Whitman _____

_____

Antonio López de Santa Anna _____

_____

William Travis _____

_____

Sam Houston _____

_____

James K. Polk _____

_____

George Donner _____

_____

Stephen Austin _____

_____

John O'Sullivan _____

_____

Richard Henry Dana _____

_____

Roger Taney _____

_____

Sequoya _____

_____

William Becknell _____

_____

Black Hawk _____

_____

Davy Crockett _____

_____

Daniel Webster _____

_____

Osceola _____

_____

Tippecanoe and Tyler Too _____

_____

Peggy Eaton _____

_____

Amos Kendall _____

_____

Johann A. Sutter _____

_____

Junípero Serra _____

_____

Thomas Hart Benton _____

_____

E. FILL IN THE BLANKS.

The Eaton affair provides a window into the interplay of politics and social status during the era of Jackson. When Secretary of War John Eaton married the widow Peggy Timberlake,

President Jackson gave his _____ believing it would quiet gossip about the two.

One New York politician said it reminded him of Jonathan Swift's remark about

using a _____ and then putting it on one's _____.

All the cabinet _____ joined in _____ Peggy Eaton,

especially the vice president's wife, _____.

Jackson, who despised the society ladies, said Peggy Eaton was _____.

The affair pushed Jackson and _____ further apart, and strengthened

Jackson's friendship with _____, who became vice president

during Jackson's second term.

[wives, head, chamber pot, as chaste as a virgin, Martin Van Buren, blessing, snubbing, Vice President Calhoun, Floride Calhoun]

Democratic congressional representatives from western states threatened war with Britain if American demands for Oregon territory were not met, but one observer noted that

"These _____ States, full of _____ and fast becoming full of _____, and

being so circumstanced as to have _____ which could be put to _____ by war, seem to

look upon war as a pleasant _____ or _____."

[people, nothing, excitement, enterprise, recreation, hazard, new]

F. TRUE FALSE—circle one.

1. T F By 1828, few states prohibited any class of male white citizens from voting.
2. T F In line with his belief that the winners deserve rewards, Andrew Jackson's administration sharply increased the federal budget to grant government contracts to his friends.
3. T F Andrew Jackson believed that any intelligent adult white male was qualified to serve in government office, so long as he was loyal to the party in power.
4. T F No federal administration up to 1820 had spent less money on roads and other internal improvements than Andrew Jackson's.
5. T F By 1828 most southern states were reducing their dependence on cotton production and foreign imports, developing a more diversified economy.
6. T F In 1832 many South Carolinians believed that if a state government found a federal law to be unconstitutional, the state could reject the operation of the law within the state's borders.
7. T F During a Jefferson Day dinner at the Executive Mansion, President Andrew Jackson offered a toast expressing his unreserved support of John C. Calhoun's fight for states' rights.
8. T F By 1830 the Cherokee had become independent farmers, with their own written language and formal schools for their children.
9. T F Black Fox led resistance by the Sauk people against their removal from Georgia.
10. T F Seminole led by Osceola retreated into the Everglades and from 1837 until 1842 fought against troops of the United States in Florida.
11. T F Andrew Jackson's veto of the bill extending the charter of the Second Bank of the United States was unpopular with voters, and nearly cost him the 1832 election.
12. T F In 1832 and 1833 South Carolina passed an ordinance of nullification of federal import tariffs, declaring them unenforceable in the state, prohibiting appeal to the Supreme Court of the United States, and threatening to secede if the federal law was enforced.
13. T F Many supporters of the Whig Party favored laws enforcing Sabbath observance and policing personal behavior.
14. T F Democratic Party voters demanded laws prohibiting alcohol and Sunday sports.
15. T F Roman Catholic immigrants were drawn more to the Democratic than to the Whig Party.
16. T F The French-speaking population of Quebec longed to be rescued from British colonial domination and annexed to the United States.
17. T F Daniel Webster whipped up passions for war with his stirring oratory over the border dispute between Maine and New Brunswick between 1837 and 1842.
18. T F Indians of the northwestern coast were not farmers but had a dense population and complex social life sustained by salmon and supplemented by game, berries, and wild plants.
19. T F Many Americans distrusted Roman Catholic immigrants.
20. T F Many rivers in Mexican borderlands, today the southwestern United States, empty into inland sinks where water simply evaporates, leaving alkali flats.
21. T F European diseases and the hard pace of work and discipline in Spanish missions along the coast shrank by a third California's Indian population.

22. T F After Mexican independence, cattle ranches in California traded with ships from New England, selling leather and tallow in exchange for manufactured goods.

23. T F When Mexico won independence from Spain in 1821, a sense of national identity and purpose united all of Mexican society under a strong federal government.

24. T F From 1821 to 1843 the government of Mexico banned all trade on the Santa Fe Trail, impoverishing the people of New Mexico and bringing war with the United States.

25. T F By 1830 about eight thousand people born in the United States and coming from west of the Appalachians and south of the Ohio River were residents of the Mexican state of Texas.

26. T F Texans sought statehood under the Mexican federal constitution, separate from the state of Coahuila, whose legislature met seven hundred miles from the Texas settlements.

27. T F Texans opposed General Antonio López de Santa Anna's seizure of the Mexican federal government, and expected his rule to be a disaster.

28. T F Mexican soldiers defeated an attempt by Texas President Mirabeau Lamar to seize Santa Fe, New Mexico, and extend the boundaries of Texas to the Pacific Ocean.

29. T F The "partisan" in charge of Hudson's Bay Company fur trappers led his party into the wilderness dressed in a broadcloth suit, white shirt, and high crowned beaver hat.

30. T F Fur trappers liked to cook their food over chips of dried buffalo manure, saying the fire gave a delicious peppery flavor to roasting meat.

31. T F The practical frontier medical knowledge of the western fur trappers, and their meticulous sanitary habits even in the wilderness, saved Indians from many diseases.

32. T F From 1840 until the mid-1870s, Oregon was popularly known as the Great American Desert and settlers avoided it.

33. T F Although early missionaries to Oregon made little headway at converting Indians, their reports to supporters back east attracted thousands to establish farms in the territory.

34. T F John Tyler, the Whig candidate for vice president who succeeded President Harrison, fought to block Democratic Party efforts to annex Texas and Oregon.

35. T F Caravans traveling to Oregon went for a hundred miles along the Platte River, described as being too thick to drink and too thin to plow.

G. MULTIPLE CHOICE—circle one or more correct answers.

1. Among regional feelings between 1828 and 1840 were these:
   a) Settlers in the West wanted easy access to land at low prices, while leaders in the Northeast feared that westward migration would create a labor shortage and raise wages.
   b) People in Missouri were tired of having so many immigrants tramp through the state on their way to Nebraska.
   c) States with economies in which slavery had become entrenched feared that at a federal level they would be outvoted by free states.
   d) English-speaking populations feared they would eventually be outnumbered by French speakers from Canada and Louisiana, along with Spanish-speaking migrants from the far Southwest.
   e) Political and economic interests in northeastern states favored a powerful, active role for the federal government; most in the South and West did not.

2. State and federal relations with the Cherokee Nation just before the Trail of Tears included these incidents:
   a) The Seventh Cavalry was sent to fight Cherokee warriors in Georgia and the Carolinas and kill all the game in their traditional hunting lands.
   b) Chief Justice John Marshall wrote a controversial Supreme Court decision that the Cherokees were not citizens and could be moved anywhere the government chose.
   c) The legislature of Georgia declared the laws of the Cherokee Nation null and void as of June 1, 1830, and required all white residents among the Cherokee to take a state oath of allegiance.
   d) Congress appropriated funds to induce Native Americans to move west of the Mississippi under new treaties.
   e) A portion of the Cherokee nation signed the Treaty of New Echota, giving up all lands in Georgia, which the rest of the Cherokee were unable to reverse.

3. Opponents of the Second Bank of the United States included
   a) state banks that resented its regulation of their credit policies, which it accomplished by limiting the amount of money it would loan to state banks.
   b) wealthy business interests that denounced the Bank for issuing paper money, insisting that all debts should be paid in gold or silver only.
   c) southern congressional representatives who claimed that the Bank's lending policies were allowing free African Americans to purchase homes in white neighborhoods.
   d) President Jackson, who charged that the Bank's charter was a taxpayer subsidy of the private share-holders.
   e) politicians who suspected it of using its resources to subvert democracy and the will of the people; and it did bribe many well-known public figures.

4. In response to the nullfication crisis in 1832 and 1833, President Andrew Jackson
   a) announced that as president of the United States he had to respect the right of each state to do as it pleased, even to leave the Union.
   b) requested and secured from Congress a Force Bill granting him powers to use the army to compel obedience to federal laws.
   c) placed South Carolina under martial law and ordered John Calhoun shot by firing squad.
   d) supported a compromise tariff bill introduced by Henry Clay to conciliate southern opposition to protective tariffs.
   e) denounced the nullifiers for "wickedness, madness and folly . . . in their attempt to destroy themselves and our union."

5. Conditions that have been presented as contributing to causing the Panic of 1837 included
   a) rampant inflation caused by unrealistic wage increases that new and powerful trade unions demanded from their employers.
   b) Nicholas Biddle's effort to demonstrate the importance of the Second Bank of the United States to the economy by tightening credit drastically.
   c) insider trading in the unregulated stock markets of the time, which created paper corporations that collapsed and took the savings of millions with them.
   d) careless loans by state banks to land speculators, which produced a feverishly booming economy that inevitably crashed when credit tightened.
   e) the Specie Circular issued by the United States Treasury requiring payment for government land in gold or silver, a policy that forced western banks to borrow gold from eastern banks.

6. The Democratic Party, forming after the administration of Andrew Jackson,
   a) passed some of the first prohibition laws in the nation, and attempted without success to win a constitutional amendment banning the manufacture of alcohol.
   b) advocated laissez-faire in economics, combined with local control and states' rights on most issues of public or national concern.
   c) tried to secure support of "mechanicks" and wage earners in the cities, but often lost ground to workingmen's parties there.
   d) never appealed to the mass of small free farmers, who generally found the Democrats too radical and were more comfortable with the Whigs.
   e) was the party more prepared to oppose interference with slavery.

7. The philosophy of Manifest Destiny took different forms, among them
   a) a belief in the obligation of the United States to absorb the entire continent of North America for the great experiment of liberty and self-government.
   b) a call for patience and restraint, teaching that God would in due time manifest His plans for the United States if the nation refrained from presumptuous military adventures.
   c) a sense of cultural and racial superiority.
   d) the extension of a fraternal welcome to descendants of loyalists who had fled to Canada after the American Revolution, and to the Roman Catholic inhabitants of Quebec.
   e) a belief in the right and duty of the federal government to take over, by military conquest if necessary, the territory of both neighboring republics and colonial possessions.

8. Up until 1846, the words "Oregon Territory" referred to
   a) a strip of land on the banks of the Columbia River.
   b) an area of land north of California and south of Alaska inhabited by Tlingit, Haida, Kwakiutl, Chinook, Salish, and Tilamook.
   c) a region on the northern Pacific coast contested by Russian and British fur trappers, both of whom abandoned all claims once settlers moved in from the United States.
   d) the only portion of North America claimed by China, which valued the coastline for obtaining sea otter skins.
   e) land in the Pacific Northwest subject to conventions and renewals by the United States and Great Britain, establishing joint occupation without consulting the inhabitants.

9. The Mexican borderlands up until 1845 were the home of
   a) small farmers raising wheat and cotton.
   b) Kiowa, Commanche, and other nomadic tribes who hunted buffalo and in the late 1600s had acquired horses from Mexico.
   c) Zuni, Hopi, and Acomi who lived in adobe brick villages, raising corn and beans on irrigated land on top of mesas or built into cliffsides.
   d) cattle companies from the United States that pastured their herds on Mexican land, fighting gun battles with both Mexican landowners and Indians.
   e) *mestizos*, of mixed European and Indian ancestry.

10. After independence the government of Mexico
    a) was dominated by a series of military dictators who sold virgin land to investors from the United States, then confiscated the estates once they were developed and productive.
    b) rotated between centralists, who wanted rule by a strong president, and federalists who favored republican government sharing power with the states.
    c) evicted friars and sold California mission lands to *rancheros*, who developed large cattle ranches, while Indians returned to their ancestral homes.
    d) was dominated by a newly enfranchised class of small farmers who had organized and fought the revolution against Spanish rule.
    e) sought under centrist presidents to attract foreign investment and settlers to underdeveloped northern areas, a policy that federalists generally opposed.

11. Immigrants to Texas from the United States were
    a) attracted to the warm and well-watered eastern part of the territory, with soil ideal for growing cotton by slave labor.
    b) in some cases provided for by terms of Austin's land grant that each settler would convert to the Roman Catholic faith and receive a large tract of land.
    c) in some cases offered a large tract under state law of Coahuila-Texas, inviting any Christian who would swear allegiance to Mexico to settle its unoccupied lands.
    d) opposed to a law of Coahuila-Texas for gradual emancipation of slaves and a later decree by the president of Mexico abolishing slavery.
    e) respectful of the Consitution of 1824, disdainful of the failure of promised social reforms, and increasingly convinced of their cultural and social superiority.

12. Initial events in the succession of incidents leading to the independence of Texas from Mexico included
    a) the arrest and imprisonment in Mexico City of the best-known Texan leaders, who were kept chained to a wall of their cell and permitted no visitors.
    b) rebellion throughout Mexico against the rule of Santa Anna, who had abolished local control over all state governments.
    c) an attack by a Texan militia in and around San Antonio that drove Mexican troops south of the Rio Grande River.

d) a "Declaration of Causes" endorsing the republican principles of the Mexican Constitution and pledging continued loyalty to Mexico.

e) a declaration of Texas as an independent republic, with a constitution that accepted slavery as a legal institution.

13. After four thousand Mexican troops under Santa Anna captured the Alamo, killing 187 Texans,

a) most Texas settlers abandoned the fight for independence and sought to reach an accommodation with Santa Anna.

b) Texas rallied to the cry "Remember the Alamo," and the slaughter of three hundred prisoners at Goliad added to their anger.

c) Texas Rangers won an unbroken string of daring victories in guerrilla warfare with the more numerous Mexican armies under Santa Anna.

d) Sam Houston retreated east with the remaining Texas army, while settlers fled in panic and his officers discussed mutiny.

e) Santa Anna in pursuit of Houston's troops divided his army into three columns, and when two of them were trapped west of the flooded Brazos River, Houston defeated Santa Anna's column near San Jacinto.

14. The independence of Texas as a republic no longer part of Mexico was secured by

a) the Treaty of Velasco, ending the conflict with President Santa Anna and confirming the independence of the new republic.

b) the Treaty of Nuestra Señora de Los Angeles, which defined the western boundary of Texas as the Rio Grande River.

c) renewed immigration, including group colonization schemes that settled Germans near San Antonio.

d) President Andrew Jackson's prompt reliance on the Monroe Doctrine to extend United States military protection against any Mexican attempt to retake Texas.

e) diplomatic recognition of Texas by Britain and France, secured by the republic's second president, Mirabeau Lamar.

15. Fur trade in the Rocky Mountains and the far Northwest drew

a) the Hudson's Bay Company, chartered in 1670, operating out of headquarters at Fort Vancouver on the Columbia River.

b) French *coureurs de bois* who moved west from Quebec and continued to dominate the trade to the interior of the continent until after the Civil War.

c) a consortium of trading posts licensed by the government, with start-up capital loaned by the Second Bank of the United States.

d) trappers of Anglo, Mexican, or mixed white and Indian ancestry, many of them married or attached to Indian women.

e) the American Fur Company, operating out of St. Louis, Missouri, and trading with free agents once a year at a rendezvous in the West.

16. The decision to annex the Republic of Texas to the United States was

a) demanded by the Democratic Party platform of James Polk's campaign, and firmly opposed by Henry Clay, who became less firm during the campaign.

b) eventually accepted even by Whig opponents from fear of British intervention in Texas.

c) rejected by the voters of Texas in a surprise referendum in 1845.

d) accomplished by a joint resolution of Congress, requiring a majority of both Houses, rather than by a treaty, requiring two-thirds approval in the Senate.

e) vetoed by the outgoing President John Tyler, but the new president recalled the bill and signed it into law in December 1845.

17. Settlers migrating overland to Oregon territory in the 1840s

a) were such individualists that each family traveled on its own, often going several days without seeing anyone else.

b) brought with them oxen, dairy cattle, bacon, flour, and sugar.

c) crossed the Great Plains and Rocky Mountains in the famous Conestoga wagon.

d) covered ten to twenty miles a day, traveling in caravans of about a thousand people in four consecutive divisions.

e) generally were tolerated by Plains Indians, who traded game for clothing and ammunition as long as the caravans passed quickly through.

H. ESSAY QUESTIONS OR ORAL REPORTS

1. Americans in Andrew Jackson's day, and numbers of historians since, have considered him a champion of what is sometimes called the "common man." What did that phrase mean at the time? What would a supporter today of a democratic and egalitarian politics say of Jackson's policies? This question allows you to do something historians are generally wary of doing—judging the past by present standards—but try to incorporate into your essay an understanding of what democracy and equality meant in the era of Jackson.

2. Trace the relationship of Mexican national politics to the eventual independence of Texas and its annexation to the United States. What form of government did Mexico have after it won independence from Spain? What classes in Mexico began the revolution, and what classes led at the end? Who was in power when immigration from the United States was first invited? What was the advantage of that immigration from Mexico's viewpoint? Which parties in Mexican politics did the Texas settlers align with? Why? Explain why settlers invited as a result of centralist policy became alienated from centralist government. What differences of opinion existed within the Texas settlements, for example between Stephen Austin and Sam Houston?

3. Assemble a detailed account of any overland pioneer movement in the 1840s, such as the missionaries sent to Oregon, mass migration along the Oregon Trail, the Donner Party trip to California, or another group or event of your choice. Present a summary of where the individuals involved came from, what motivated them to go, whether the results on arrival fulfilled the original purpose, and why or why not.

4. Prepare a written argument against annexation of Texas by the United States in the 1840s. Take up the position of a Democrat or a Whig, a northerner, a southerner, a westerner, or a resident of any more specific region that was opposed.

5. Detail the effect of the nineteenth-century northwestern fur trade on communities where fur trappers lived, equipped themselves, and spent their money, and on peoples living in the regions where trapping took place.

Toward Disunion   13

A. TERMS

sectional loyalty _____
_____
_____

involuntary servitude _____
_____
_____

popular sovereignty _____
_____
_____

Border Ruffians _____
_____
_____

Beecher's Bibles _____
_____
_____

civil disorder _____
_____
_____

safe conduct _____
_____
_____

amphibious landing _____
_____
_____

upward mobility _____
_____
_____

vigilance committee _____
_____
_____

_____
_____

B. PHOTOGRAPHS

1. Give several reasons why cholera has not, in recent times, periodically infected millions of people in the United States, as it did in 1832, 1848, and 1867.

2. Are any of these images accurate? How do you know? Are poverty and exploitation of British workers a good argument for the claim that slavery is a more humane system of labor? If so, would it have been desirable to extend to British workers the benefits of slavery? If not, what should be done about either slavery or poverty?

These 1841 proslavery illustrations juxtapose well cared-for African American slaves next to unemployed British workers living in poverty; other comparisons involved the contented southern slave and the northern "wage slaves" working longer hours and living in misery. (*Courtesy, New York Public Library*)

In Thomas Moran's painting *Slave Hunt*, fugitive slaves flee through the swamps. (*Courtesy, The Philbrook Museum*)

C. VOCABULARY

proviso _____

_____

manifesto _____

_____

homogenous _____

_____

xenophobic _____

_____

filibuster _____

_____

insurrection _____

_____

nativist _____

_____

Compromise of 1850 _____

_____

referendum _____

_____

Los Diablos Tejanos _____

_____

free soilers _____

_____

Know-Nothings _____

_____

Fugitive Slave Act _____

_____

_____

pauper _____

_____

_____

D. INDIVIDUALS

Zachary Taylor _____

_____

William Walker _____

_____

John Slidell _____

_____

Charles Sumner _____

_____

Winfield Scott _____

_____

John C. Frémont _____

_____

Robert Barnwell Rhett _____

_____

William Henry Seward _____

_____

Levi Coffin _____

_____

Stephen Kearny _____

_____

Dred Scott _____

_____

_____

Harriet Beecher Stowe _____

_____

_____

Harriet Tubman _____

_____

_____

David Atchison _____

_____

_____

Lewis Cass _____

_____

_____

Henry "Box" Brown _____

_____

_____

Millard Fillmore _____

_____

_____

John Hughes _____

_____

_____

John Brown _____

_____

_____

Stephen A. Douglas _____

_____

_____

Henry Ward Beecher _____

_____

_____

Uncle Tom _____

_____

_____

Franklin Pierce _____

_____

_____

E. TRUE FALSE—circle one.

1. T F Representative Abraham Lincoln of Illinois challenged President Polk's claim that Mexico had attacked United States soldiers on United States soil.
2. T F The war against Mexico was so unpopular that the federal government had difficulty finding enough volunteers to fill the necessary army ranks.

3. T F President Polk wanted a small-scale war with Mexico and a quick victory since he feared that either Winfield Scott or Zachary Taylor, each of them a prominent commander, might become a popular Whig candidate for president.

4. T F During the Mexican War, some settlers declared the independence of the Republic of California while Commodore Robert Stockton declared the region a part of the United States.

5. T F During the war in the late 1840s between the United States and Mexico, Texas Rangers spread terror by gutting women, shooting old men and children, and hanging civilians.

6. T F In the 1848 presidential election, the two major parties presented themselves in the North as sympathetic to restricting slavery and in the South as friendly to that region's concerns.

7. T F As production of gold grew from 1849 to 1852 and increasing numbers of people came to take their share, earnings of miners soared.

8. T F Following the Mexican War, Texans claimed Santa Fe, New Mexico, as part of their state, and when the United States army commander ignored their claim they threatened to seize it by force.

9. T F In 1850, the House of Representatives took sixty-three rounds of voting to decide on a speaker of the House.

10. T F Stephen Douglas, a Democratic senator from Illinois, brought to his political career the conviction that slavery was morally wrong.

11. T F The Fugitive Slave Act of 1850 provided that a federal commissioner who decided in favor of an owner claiming a slave would receive a fee larger than that for a decision that an alleged fugitive was not a slave.

12. T F Rallies in New York, New Orleans, and Boston denounced the Compromise of 1850, each demanding that the region it was located in secede from the Union.

13. T F The Chicago City Council declared the Fugitive Slave Act of 1850 in violation of the federal Constitution and the laws of God.

14. T F Refugees from failed revolutions in central Europe in the 1840s were refused entry to the United States, since the government defined them as potential subversives.

15. T F The convention of the Free Soil Party in 1852 labeled slavery "a sin against God and a crime against man."

16. T F Most immigrants in the 1840s and 1850s settled in free states, since competition with slave labor offered little opportunity; this increased the differences between the North and the South in the years before the Civil War.

17. T F In 1856 the new Republican Party contested its third presidential election.

18. T F Preston Brooks was one of the few southern congressmen to support abolitionists, and maintained a devoted friendship with Senator Charles Sumner of Massachusetts.

19. T F Lincoln criticized Douglas for his indifference to the moral implications of slavery, his willingness to accept slaveholding whenever and wherever the voters favored it.

20. T F In his debates with Abraham Lincoln in 1858, Douglas denied that the United States was "made for white men."

F. MULTIPLE CHOICE—circle one or more correct answers.

1. Miners who went to California during the initial years of the gold rush
   a) lived in luxury, eating every kind of delicacy their new-found wealth could buy.
   b) found that all the land was owned by wealthy *Californios*, so that they had to labor as peons for a few pennies a day while the owners of vast estates got the profit.
   c) spent their days up to their knees in icy water, digging in gravel, or manipulating heavy equipment to try to obtain a small amount of gold.
   d) lived in crude shacks, made bread on a hot stone, and lived on pork and beans washed down with bitter coffee.
   e) seldom bathed or washed their clothes, and dosed themselves with quinine and opium for the diarrhea and scurvy that afflicted them.

2. Henry Clay's proposed compromise over slavery, federal territory, and admission of new states to the Union included these provisions:
   a) California would be admitted as a free state, while no restriction on slavery was to apply to the remainder of the Mexican Cession.
   b) In exchange for the suppression of the Underground Railroad, all slaves would be emancipated by the end of the century.
   c) Slave trading was to be abolished in the District of Columbia, but ownership of slaves in the District would continue.
   d) Congress would not impose any restrictions or regulations on interstate trade in slaves.
   e) Annual conferences would be held at various points along the banks of the Ohio River seeking understanding between northerners and southerners.

3. John C. Calhoun's response to Henry Clay's proposed compromise asserted that
   a) South Carolina had never really wanted to be part of the United States in the first place, and joined only because blacks outnumbered whites by six to one.
   b) northern policies had created a great centralized machine in Washington that would crush the South.
   c) only if every state agreed to legalize slavery, and to make slaves of chronically unemployed white men, could the Union be preserved.
   d) the nation was already dividing in two, as the division of Protestant churches into separate northern and southern denominations demonstrated.
   e) southern secession could be avoided only by equal division of the territories into slave and non-slave states, and a constitutional amendment guaranteeing the South equality with the North.

4. Daniel Webster's main points in support of Henry Clay's proposed compromise included these:
   a) The territory ceded by Mexico was by geography and climate unsuited to slavery, so there was no need to offend the South by excluding slavery from it by law.
   b) The frequent financial contributions he had received from prominent southerners demonstrated that sectional differences could be overcome.
   c) Southerners were justified in complaining about the hindrances to enforcement of the fugitive slave laws.
   d) Peaceful division of the Union would be impossible.
   e) Even if Illinois and Ohio insisted on undermining the fugitive slave laws, Massachusetts and New Hampshire would be true friends of the South.

5. These statements are true of immigration to the United States:
   a) Before 1830, strict laws prohibited anyone not born in the United States from moving here.
   b) Between 1830 and 1840, immigration rose sharply.
   c) After 1845, large numbers of immigrants arrived from Ireland and Germany, with smaller migrations from Scandinavia and Great Britain other than Ireland.
   d) Immigrants entering the United States swelled by 1850 to three hundred thousand a year.
   e) Immigration to the United States expanded after the repeal of federal laws forbidding it.

6. The Irish potato famine, which determined millions of Irish to immigrate to the United States,
   a) was caused by a fungus that rotted potatoes, leaving the poor without food.
   b) came after several years in a row with hardly any rain.
   c) did not move the British government to supply adequate emergency supplies of food to the starving Irish.
   d) was discovered many years later to have come about because repeated potato crops had used up certain needed nutrients in the soil.
   e) reduced the population of Ireland by twenty-five percent from 1845 to 1851, half of that by death from starvation, the other half by the flight of Irish to other lands.

7. The Kansas-Nebraska Act, passed in 1854,
   a) settled the angry passions left over from the debate over the Compromise of 1850.
   b) put an end to whatever reconciliation the Compromise of 1850 had achieved.

c) repealed the provision of the Missouri Compromise prohibiting slavery north of 36° 30'.

d) could have increased the value of land in which Senator Douglas had invested.

e) closed the Great Plains to settlement, reserving it for Indian nations only.

8. The shift in party allegiances in the election of 1854
   a) meant the demise of the Whig Party, which virtually ceased to exist.
   b) lost the Democratic Party enough of its former voting constituency in the North to bring the defeat of the majority of its congressmen from the free states.
   c) eliminated the American Party from national politics by stunning defeats.
   d) consolidated the Republican Party as a national force founded on Free Soil Party voters along with disaffected Whigs and antislavery Democrats.
   e) brought brutal suppression of the workingmen's parties formed in the 1830s.

9. Among people passionately involved in the fight over whether Kansas was to become a free or a slave state, possible outcomes of the struggle that one side or the other thought, feared, or hoped for included
   a) the extension of slavery all the way to the Pacific if the proslavery forces won in Kansas.
   b) the reintroduction of slavery to New England if a large part of its population moved to Kansas.
   c) an alliance between militant abolitionists like John Brown and the Oglala Lakota nation.
   d) the closing off of the territories from slavery if the antislavery forces won in Kansas.
   e) the pushing out of free white farmers from Kansas along with whatever other territories might become open to slavery.

10. Adjusting his position to where he was campaigning in the 1858 Illinois race for United States senator, Abraham Lincoln claimed at one time or another that
    a) the Fugitive Slave Law must be repealed and the interstate slave trade prohibited.
    b) "I am not in favor of bringing about in any way the social and political equality of the black and white races."
    c) Americans should "discard all this quibbling . . . " about whether one man or another, one race or another, is inferior, "and unite as one people, throughout this land."
    d) slavery could continue indefinitely in the states where it existed because it had supported the economies of those states for many years.
    e) Republicans intended to "arrest the further spread" of slavery until it was "in the course of ultimate extinction"; the government "cannot endure half slave and half free."

11. The Underground Railroad was
    a) a secret coordinating body for railway owners seeking government subsidies.
    b) a small network of safe houses where fugitive slaves could find temporary refuge before moving on toward a free state or Canada.
    c) organized by railroad workers as a clandestine body after their unions were outlawed.
    d) the work of Harriet Tubman and Levi Coffin, among others.
    e) an effort that has won a permanent place in the history of the struggle against slavery.

G. ESSAY QUESTIONS OR ORAL REPORTS

1. From a sampling of campaign speeches, political documents, or newspaper comments in northern states concerning the disposal of lands seized from Mexico, discuss how far the comments expressed moral concerns and how much they demonstrate that banning slavery in the new lands would benefit white northerners economically and socially.

2. Compare the record of enforcement of the fugitive slave laws with the enforcement of laws that regarded international slave trading as piracy, punishable by death. Was anyone ever actually hanged for slave trading? What response to each of these laws was taken by various state governments, and by federal officials in different departments and areas of the country?

3. Sampling a number of supporters of slavery who lived in states where it already existed, explain why they resisted so fiercely the banning of slavery from the newer territories. If slavery was safe within their states, what economic interests or social and ideological concerns made them worry about its prohibition elsewhere?

4. Trace the history of anti-Catholic prejudice in the United States, from its origins in the religious wars of Europe, through the Spanish Armada and British conflicts with Spain and France, to the late colonial period and the American Revolution, and then through relevant episodes covered in this chapter.

The Civil War 14

A. TERMS

federal installations _____

_____

_____

conscription _____

_____

_____

commander-in-chief _____

_____

_____

diplomatic recognition _____

_____

_____

tactical dexterity _____

_____

_____

B. PHOTOGRAPHS

1. Explain each of the images in the cartoon on the next page. Identify each candidate, the candidate's dancing partner, the important points of his platform, and how the person represented by the featured musician relates to the proceedings in general.

_____

_____

_____

_____

_____

_____

_____

_____

_____

_____

_____

2. The twentieth-century black militant Malcolm X, asked at some time prior to his pilgrimage to Mecca whether there was any white man he respected, would reply "John Brown." Frederick Douglass remarked that Brown's commitment to abolition was greater than Douglass's own. Citizens of Harpers Ferry drove Brown's little force into an engine house until marines could capture him. Virginia hanged John Brown as a traitor. Write either an indictment of John Brown or a eulogy for him, written from the perspective of someone living at the time he lived, using studies and sources of facts available to you today. A particularly helpful book on Brown has been edited by John Stauffer (Brandywine Press, 2003).

C. VOCABULARY

homestead _____

_____

arsenal _____

_____

daguerreotype _____

_____

ironclad _____

_____

contraband _____

_____

greenbacks _____

_____

sanitation _____

_____

chloroform _____

_____

copperheads _____

_____

_____

D. INDIVIDUALS

John Brown _____

_____

Mary Chesnut _____

_____

Joseph Hooker _____

_____

Robert E. Lee _____

_____

_____

Jefferson Davis _____

_____

George B. McClellan _____

_____

William S. Rosecrans _____

_____

Irvin McDowell _____

_____

Jubal Early _____

_____

Philip Sheridan _____

_____

William Tecumseh Sherman _____

_____

Nathan Bedford Forrest _____

_____

Ambrose E. Burnside _____

_____

John C. Breckinridge _____

_____

John Bell Hood _____

_____

P. T. G. Beauregard _____

_____

John Bell _____

_____

_____

Joseph E. Johnston _____

_____

_____

George G. Meade _____

_____

_____

James Longstreet _____

_____

_____

Benjamin Butler _____

_____

_____

Clement L. Vallandigham _____

_____

_____

Thomas J. Jackson _____

_____

_____

Ulysses S. Grant _____

_____

_____

J. E. B. Stuart _____

_____

_____

Elizabeth Blackwell _____

_____

_____

E. TRUE FALSE—circle one.

1. T F The Republican Party platform of 1860 appealed to northern race prejudice, through measures that would settle white homesteaders in the West, excluding large plantations, slaves, and, at least by implication, free African Americans.

2. T F After the 1860 presidential election, a convention in South Carolina requested that Lincoln clarify his position toward slavery in the states where it was then legal, and suggested it might vote to secede from the Union if his response was not satisfactory.

3. T F The Confederate Constitution of 1861 was in large part modeled on the United States Constitution of 1787, but explicitly protected "the institution of Negro slavery."

4. T F Abraham Lincoln made a triumphal entry into Washington, D.C., for his inauguration.

5. T F Major Robert Anderson, commanding officer at Fort Sumter, opened an artillery barrage on South Carolina militia in Charleston harbor, provoking a Confederate counterattack.

6. T F President Lincoln issued a call in April 1861 for seventy-five thousand militia volunteers to serve for ninety days in suppressing insurrection against the United States.

7. T F Military conflict between Union and Confederate forces began on July 21, 1861, at the Battle of Bull Run in eastern Virginia.

8. T F Secretary of State Seward announced that because secession was illegal, Confederate soldiers captured by the Union army would be prosecuted for treason and insurrection.

9. T F General George B. McClellan did an expert job of training, drilling, and organizing the Army of the Potomac, but Lincoln was disappointed at McClellan's hesitation to take the army into combat.

10. T F An important victory for the federal blockade of the Confederate coastline was the capture of Roanoke Island in North Carolina by a Union army under command of General Ambrose E. Burnside.

11. T F The *Trent* affair began when two Confederate agents under British diplomatic passports were captured outside a historic mansion in the New Jersey state capital.

12. T F For the manufacture of gunpowder, United States military forces during the Civil War depended on imports of saltpeter from India, which was ruled by Britain.

13. T F One argument for freeing slaves, as a wartime policy, was to deprive the Confederacy of badly needed labor to replace that of white men called up for military service.

14. T F The Homestead Act of 1860 offered a 160-acre plot of federal land to any man or woman who lived on it for five years and improved it by cultivation or building.

15. T F Land grant colleges got their name because they were built in various states on land granted by the federal government for the purpose of establishing schools.

16. T F The Emancipation Proclamation abolished slavery throughout the United States.

17. T F Democrats who favored immediate peace with the Confederacy denounced a war of emancipation as an assault on the freedoms of white Americans.

18. T F Rank and file Confederate soldiers denounced draft exemptions for large slaveowners as a sign that the Confederacy was run for the benefit of the rich.

19. T F In the northern states the Democratic Party ran a racist campaign in 1864, attacking emancipation, denouncing Lincoln as wasting white lives in the cause of black freedom.

20. T F Lee retired from the Battle of Gettysburg with almost as many troops in the Army of Northern Virginia as when the battle began.

21. T F In the defense of the federal garrison at Milliken's Bend on the Mississippi River above Vicksburg, soldiers of African descent demonstrated their fighting ability.

22. T F In the fall of 1863 northern public opinion, inspired by the New York draft riots and the fighting around Vicksburg, turned sharply against abolition of slavery.

23. T F Copperhead victories in the elections for governor in Ohio and Pennsylvania undermined support for Lincoln's government in 1863.

24. T F A Unionist majority in eastern Tennessee lived under Confederate military occupation until the summer of 1863.

25. T F In May 1864 Confederate cavalry under General Jubal Early reached the northern suburbs of Washington, D.C.

26. T F In 1864 Maryland and Missouri voted for the Democratic presidential candidate George McClellan, while Delaware, New Jersey, and Kentucky voted to reelect Lincoln.

27. T F The demands of the Civil War strained northern industry beyond endurance, while wartime need spurred a great growth in southern manufacturing.

28. T F One measure no Confederate official or general would ever consider during the entire war was enlisting African Americans as soldiers in the rebel army.

F. MATCHING Match the name of each battle listed below with its significance to the course of the war.

___Fredericksburg   f) Emancipation Proclamation issued after Lee's invasion turned back

___Vicksburg   d) defeat of Lee's last invasion of the North after three-day battle

___Antietam   a) slaughter of thousands of Union soldiers in an assault that accomplished nothing

____Atlanta

m) clear-cut victory for Confederate forces showed that the war would be long

____Chancellorsville

j) stopped Confederate attempt to chase federal army out of Tennessee

____First Bull Run

h) McClellan moved slowly, fought cautiously, outmaneuvered by Lee

____Petersburg

l) sealed off one of the last remaining Confederate ports in 1864

____Wilderness

c) Lee out-thinks, out-fights, and out-flanks Joseph Hooker

____Gettysburg

e) broke the last Confederate position on the Mississippi River

____Missionary Ridge

g) the fighting there aided in securing Union control of Chattanooga

____Mobile Bay

k) Confederate attempt to reenter eastern Tennessee was barely repulsed

____Shiloh

n) heavy Union losses, but the army pressed forward instead of retreating

____Peninsular Campaign

b) cost the Confederacy its main transportation hub and a lot of its industry

____Chickamauga Creek

i) last major battle, ending with Lee's flight, followed by surrender

G. MULTIPLE CHOICE—circle one or more correct answers.

1. In the division of the popular and electoral votes among the four major candidates for president of the United States in 1860,
   a) Lincoln won a majority of the popular vote and three quarters of the Electoral College.
   b) Stephen Douglas won the second largest number of popular votes, but took the smallest number of votes in the Electoral College.
   c) Lincoln won the largest number of popular votes and a huge majority in the Electoral College.
   d) John C. Breckinridge won eighteen percent of the popular vote, and John Bell even less, but each won more votes in the Electoral College than Douglas.
   e) Lincoln finished in last place in the popular vote, but won a majority of votes in the Electoral College.

2. Between the election of November 1860 and Lincoln's inauguration in March 1861,
   a) seven states from South Carolina to Texas declared that they were no longer part of the Union.
   b) Virginia, Tennessee, North Carolina, and Arkansas joined the Confederacy.
   c) President James Buchanan denied that states had a legal right to secede, but said that he could find no way to stop them.
   d) Confederate troops in Charleston, South Carolina, fired on Fort Sumter.
   e) the Republican leader William Seward described President Buchanan as having announced that he had a duty to enforce the law unless anyone objected.

3. Upon his becoming president, Lincoln's initial response to secession included
   a) immediate enlistment of one million soldiers to invade the seceded states.
   b) a promise not to interfere with slavery in states where it existed, though he rejected a proposal to allow slavery in territories south of the Missouri Compromise line.
   c) endorsement of a secret proposal to go to war with France and Spain, as a tactic to reunite the country.
   d) securing federal installations located in seceded states, so that in event of armed conflict the Confederacy would be the aggressor.
   e) resupplying the federal garrison at Fort Sumter, South Carolina, and notifying state authorities of his intention to do so.

4. Among the northernmost states that allowed slavery as of 1861,
   a) Missouri's governor remained loyal to the Union, but rebels took over most of the state and held Missouri throughout the war.
   b) militias for and against secession were organized in Kentucky, but most residents of the state remained loyal to the Union.
   c) western North Carolina and eastern Tennessee were mostly loyal to the Union, rebelling against state governments and sending volunteers to the federal army.
   d) Massachusetts volunteers heading for Washington to defend the capital against Confederate forces were enthusiastically greeted as they passed through Maryland.
   e) support for secession from the state of Virginia was strong in the mountainous western region: federal troops and local Unionists drove out Confederate forces.

5. The first Battle of Bull Run, also known as Manassas,
   a) resulted in a stunning Union victory that led to hopes for an early end to the war.
   b) was fought on both sides by soldiers who lacked training and experience.
   c) gave General Thomas Jackson the nickname "Stonewall" for keeping his brigade of Virginia soldiers steady in breaking a federal assault.
   d) made Robert E. Lee famous as commanding general of Confederate forces.
   e) ended in a defeat of federal forces, at the end of a hard day's fighting by both sides.

6. Material advantages held by states loyal to the Union against the Confederacy included
   a) a population of nine million in the seceded states, of whom a third consisted of slaves.
   b) a tradition of military service and training, which produced a hardened combat force more powerful than the southern sense of honor could deliver.
   c) a diverse economy with abundant industry, also self-sufficient in food.
   d) the sympathy of the British government, which because it had patrolled the Atlantic for fifty years to suppress the slave trade would never think of aiding the Confederacy.
   e) a navy to deploy in a blockade of Confederate ports, while the Confederacy depended on foreign trade to sustain its economy.

7. Years of fighting in northern Virginia between Washington and Richmond changed little, while in the western theater of the Civil War, by the end of 1862
   a) Confederate cavalry raided deep into northern Ohio and Illinois, greeted by people holding strong southern sympathies.
   b) Union forces moved up the Tennessee and Cumberland rivers from Illinois, taking forts Henry and Donelson and the city of Nashville, and winning the Battle of Shiloh.
   c) Texas, Louisiana, and Arkansas voted to rejoin the United States, prevented only by Confederate military occupation under General Albert Sidney Johnston.
   d) New Orleans fell to a Union naval force that cut off Confederate river traffic on the Mississippi from the Gulf of Mexico.
   e) a Confederate invasion of Kentucky under General Braxton Bragg was turned back at Perryville in October.

8. Confederate hopes for diplomatic recognition from Britain and France depended on
   a) powerful Confederate military victories, showing that the South could win.
   b) dependence of British textile industries on imported cotton, which could motivate Britain to break the blockade of southern ports.
   c) French intervention in Mexico, which would gain from a permanent split in the United States and Confederate support of the French presence in Mexico.
   d) whether slavery became an issue of the war; Britain could not openly support the Confederacy if the Union government made emancipation a war policy.
   e) large bribes demanded by French government officials from Confederate diplomats, privately referred to as the "little x, y, z affair."

9. The evolution of United States military policy toward slavery included these steps:
    a) On April 3, 1861, Lincoln issued an executive order that any slaves encountered by federal military forces would be "henceforth and forever free."
    b) General Benjamin Butler took in fugitive slaves, arguing that as property of rebels, they were "contraband of war"; and since Union officers refused to hold them as property, they should be considered free.
    c) In 1862 Congress prohibited the return of fugitive slaves to their owners, then offered financial support to any state adopting a gradual end to slavery.
    d) Fugitive slaves reaching federal lines were organized into caravans and sent to Lawrence, Kansas, for resettlement on reservations.
    e) A militia act in late 1862 authorized the president to enlist men of African ancestry into the military.

10. Draft riots in New York City in 1863 were motivated in part by
    a) hostility among Irish immigrant laborers toward New York residents of African descent, many of whom sought the same low-paid jobs as the Irish.
    b) anger at conscription for military service and the belief that only the poorer classes were actually called up.
    c) resentment toward employers who were hostile to labor unions.
    d) a determination to have the government of the United States submit to the Pope.
    e) wrath directed at Protestant churches.

11. Popular resentment by civilians of Confederate government policy took the form of
    a) massive nonviolent antiwar protests in Atlanta, New Orleans, and Richmond.
    b) resistance to decrees that farmers must turn over a portion of crops, meat, and dairy products to the government.
    c) bread riots in major southern cities, where women invaded shops selling food and took whatever they needed.
    d) repeated assassination attempts targeting members of Jefferson Davis's cabinet.
    e) a virtual secession from Confederate law by areas opposed to conscription.

12. In his campaigns in command of the Army of the Potomac, Grant
    a) was so arrogant that he ignored direction from President Lincoln and at times refused even to speak to his commander-in-chief.
    b) continued his offensive against the Army of Northern Virginia after each battle, regardless of his losses in the previous fighting.
    c) paused for long periods of time between battles to reprovision his soldiers and think over what he wanted to do next.
    d) forced the Confederate forces from one defensive position to another.
    e) was racing to win victories faster than Sherman, his lifelong rival and enemy.

13. When General William Tecumseh Sherman captured Atlanta from Confederate troops,
    a) he was victorious in a long campaign of maneuvering around entrenched Confederate positions that could not be taken by frontal assault.
    b) his soldiers indiscriminately slaughtered the civilian population of the city.
    c) the victory improved Lincoln's chances of reelection by northern voters.
    d) the Confederate general Hood tried to move north and cut Sherman's supply lines to Tennessee, but Sherman decided to forget the supply lines and live off the land.
    e) the entire city was dismantled and put into storage, not to be seen again until it was pulled out for use as a backdrop in making movies eighty years later.

14. On the disposal of black prisoners of war,
    a) neither the federal command nor the Confederate officers had any interest in treating African Americans as soldiers once they were captured.
    b) federal troops taken prisoner by Confederate armies refused to live in the same prisoner-of-war camps with African American prisoners.

c) in 1863, Confederate armies refused to treat African Americans as prisoners of war, or exchange them on equal terms for white soldiers.

d) the federal government refused to exchange any prisoners unless all federal soldiers were treated the same, and this decision increased the numbers kept in prisoner compounds.

e) not until January 1865 did the Confederate government agree that all African Americans captured in battle, in federal uniform, were prisoners of war.

15. Sanitation and medical knowledge had what impact on the lives of Civil War soldiers?

a) The first cholera epidemic to reach the United States forced General McClellan to keep the Army of the Potomac in camp for most of 1862.

b) At the time the medical profession was ignorant of the microorganisms causing infection, and despite some serious attempts at teaching cleanliness to the troops, disease killed more soldiers than battlefield combat.

c) Advanced scientific and technical ability kept federal soldiers quite healthy, while Confederate soldiers, paying no attention to cleanliness, died of infectious disease.

d) The United States Sanitary Commission was organized to recruit nurses, obtain medical supplies, and teach better hygienic methods to soldiers.

e) To stop the spread of gangrene from infected wounds, physicians of that time had no measure available except amputation.

ESSAY QUESTIONS OR ORAL REPORTS

1. On the question of allowing slavery in federal territories, in the District of Columbia, and in states where slavery was prohibited, consider the applicability of constitutional guarantees, more specifically the Fifth Amendment, protecting private property from seizure or interference by the federal government. Was the Supreme Court under Chief Justice Roger Taney legally correct when it ruled that slaves were property, and that property in slaves was an individual right of the slaveowner?

2. Present an argument as to what Abraham Lincoln's own inner political motivations were during his presidency. Examine his presidential actions, the circumstances surrounding each, and the results they led to in the long term. Did he intend to abolish slavery, and use the war to bring reluctant northern public opinion around to the idea? Or was he genuinely motivated only by a desire to save the Union, speaking to questions of slavery and race only when it served the interest of federal supremacy?

3. Can a government "conceived in liberty, and dedicated to the proposition that all men are created equal" be strong enough to defend itself against insurrection and foreign enemies? What freedoms and constitutional guarantees did the Union government set aside in order to save the republic?

4. Examine the Civil War career of General George B. McClellan. Provide your own analysis of how he might better have handled his responsibility for the Army of the Potomac. Or make a case that he was following the right course. In the course of your investigation, refer to McClellan's own writings, and the writings of Lincoln and others in the government.

5. Prepare an economic overview of the world market for cotton from 1859 through 1867. In what regions worldwide was cultivation well established and where was it just beginning? Decide what the possibilities were of the Confederacy's pressuring Britain into diplomatic recognition and a naval assault against the Union blockade for the sake of keeping the flow of southern cotton to British factories.

6. Pick a battle of the Civil War and write a detailed analysis of why it began as it did, the options that each commanding officer had at critical points as the battle developed, and why each made the choices he did.

Reconstructing the South

15

A. TERMS

Freedmen's Bureau _____
_____
_____

forty acres and a mule _____
_____
_____

Reconstruction _____
_____
_____

market capitalism _____
_____
_____

gang labor _____
_____
_____

harmony of capital and labor _____
_____
_____

Black Codes _____
_____
_____

republican government _____
_____
_____

civil rights _____
_____
_____

due process of law _____
_____
_____

white supremacy _____

_____

_____

equal protection of the laws _____

_____

_____

states' rights _____

_____

_____

B. PHOTOGRAPHS

1. Look up George Washington's and Abraham Lincoln's own writings on the subject of slavery, mostly to be found in personal correspondence. Have them discuss the subject.

2. Write a summary of the formation of the Ku Klux Klan and its activity during Reconstruction. In its origins the KKK murdered Republicans, voted for Democrats, and prided itself on its resistance to the policies of the victorious United States. The revived Klan of the 1920s celebrated loyalty to the United States. It allied itself with Republicans and Democrats who supported the Eighteenth Amendment prohibiting the manufacture and sale of alcohol. And it directed much of its hatred against Roman Catholics, Jews, and immigrants from central and eastern Europe. It was white supremacist, but African Americans were not its single obsession. Write a brief essay comparing the two Klans, examining why the second Klan took on the character it did and why Catholics, Jews, the newer waves of immigrants, and violators of Prohibition were its chosen targets. Suggest why the second Klan, different in so many ways from the Klan of Reconstruction days, nonetheless thought itself to be the descendant of that first KKK.

_____

_____

_____

_____

_____

_____

_____

_____

3. Note the political climate of 1872 and the career of Thomas Nast. Then write a summary of what the cartoon on the next page represented at the time. What politics was Horace Greeley endorsing by 1872, and what was the position his political faction took toward Reconstruction? Note also that the figure standing beside the Klansman is Irish. The facial features became stereotypical for portrayals of the Irish and would survive into the popular and friendlier Maggie and Jiggs newspaper comic strip of the twentieth century. Why does Nast make the Irish into allies of the Klan? Think of events in New York City in the summer of 1863, and remember that the Irish voted Democratic.

C. VOCABULARY

Johnson's "Swing Around the Circle" _____

_____

_____

freedmen _____

_____

_____

sharecropping _____

_____

_____

peonage _____

_____

_____

impeachment _____

_____

_____

carpetbaggers _____

_____

_____

scalawags _____

_____

_____

ten-percent plan _____

_____

_____

pocket veto _____

_____

_____

terrorism _____

_____

_____

crop lien _____

_____

_____

D. INDIVIDUALS

Oliver Otis Howard _____

_____

_____

Andrew Johnson _____

_____

_____

John Wilkes Booth _____
_____
_____

Alexander Stephens _____
_____
_____

Thaddeus Stevens _____
_____
_____

Horatio Seymour _____
_____
_____

Lucy Stone _____
_____
_____

Thomas Nast _____
_____
_____

Susan B. Anthony _____
_____
_____

Elizabeth Cady Stanton _____
_____
_____

Horace Greeley _____
_____
_____

Benjamin Butler _____
_____
_____

E. TRUE FALSE—circle one.

1. T F All slaves throughout the country were officially free as of April 9, 1865, following Robert E. Lee's surrender at Appomattox.
2. T F Tennessee, according to the status the Union defined for the state, abolished slavery by law in 1863.
3. T F Most black southerners in 1870 lived in a two-parent home.
4. T F As a result of the Emancipation Proclamation, slaves became free when the Union army conquered rebel territory in which they were held as slaves.
5. T F Sharecropping was a status for freed blacks, not for white farmers.
6. T F Early after the end of the Civil War southern militia units, some wearing Confederate uniforms, patrolled the countryside in former Confederate states enforcing Black Codes.
7. T F Emancipation was bewildering for both freed slaves and their former owners.

8. T F Federal officials encouraged freed slaves to leave the plantations and take to the road.
9. T F President Andrew Johnson identified with the southern plantation owning class.
10. T F Some former slaves, knowing how helpless their former owners were at the prospect of survival by working, attempted to help them out.
11. T F The Congress elected in 1866 denied seats to southern representatives and senators elected by new southern state governments endorsed by President Johnson.
12. T F John Tyler, a former president of the United States, held a public office within the Confederacy, and if he had survived the war the Fourteenth Amendment would have barred him from federal office unless Congress removed the restriction.
13. T F Andrew Johnson's hostility to the slave-owning planter class made him friendly toward the rights of the freed slaves.
14. T F Tennessee refused to ratify the Fourteenth Amendment.
15. T F A North Carolina planter was upset when a black veteran of the Union bowed and greeted him.
16. T F Land was taken from plantation owners as a matter of federal policy, and distributed to freed slaves so they could support themselves.
17. T F James Longstreet, a former Confederate general, led opposition to Reconstruction policies, and fomented white riots in New Orleans.
18. T F Much of the political leadership among African Americans after the Civil War came from blacks who had been free since birth and were accustomed to some independence.
19. T F During Reconstruction, blacks were a minority of the voters in South Carolina.
20. T F In the 1868 elections, the Ku Klux Klan assassinated elected officials and terrorized black and white Republican voters, with the object of defeating Horatio Seymour in the presidential election.

F. MULTIPLE CHOICE—circle one or more correct answers.

1. Among the many responses of freed slaves to emancipation was
   a) an effort to establish a gang system that would continue their familiar work patterns but without rule by slaveowners.
   b) a mixture of exaltation and sadness, affection for former owners, and a desire to lash out at them.
   c) setting out on the road to find children, parents, or spouses who had been separated from them by sale years before.
   d) forming guerrilla bands who systematically looted and burned plantations.
   e) flocking to port cities seeking ships to take them back to Africa.

2. Among the responses of slaveowners to the emancipation of their human property were these:
   a) shock that slaves thought to be happy and faithful would leave, once free to do so.
   b) a determination to divide up plantations among the slaves who had worked on them.
   c) a frenzy of whippings and other violence against their slaves, taking out their bitterness and frustration at loss of the war and anger at imminent emancipation.
   d) a general desire to drive all the freed slaves into the northern states.
   e) an invitation to their former slaves to formal meetings at which the two races could get better acquainted on an equal basis.

3. Union soldiers who brought the Emancipation Proclamation to a plantation might be
   a) committed abolitionists.
   b) white racists with no interest in freeing slaves.
   c) African Americans enlisted after 1862.
   d) Santee Lakota, afraid a Confederate victory would cost them their land.
   e) whites who became abolitionists when they saw the scars on the backs of slaves.

4. The market ideology of the Republican Party, which shaped programs for freed slaves,
   a) sought to build a nation of independent, self-sufficient small farmers.
   b) insisted that private property in land should not be disturbed or redistributed.
   c) advocated a diversified southern economy, breaking dependence on cotton.

d) believed that a labor force working for wages was better than a population of families owning a piece of land and using it for subsistence.

e) expected human beings to be hungry for possessions as a main incentive in life.

5. These were among responses on the part of northern economic interests to the postwar situation in the South:
   a) Factory owners donated millions of dollars to educational and welfare programs.
   b) Missionaries from New England taught economic self-sufficiency to freed slaves.
   c) Clothing mill owners needed endless amounts of southern cotton, so they did not want to see the land used to grow food for southern families.
   d) The northern economy was hiring massive numbers of factory hands overseen by floor superintendents, shaping a workforce similar to gang labor in the southern fields.
   e) Businesses seeking to invest in southern states expected that hiring freedmen would provide them with a more loyal workforce than hiring Confederate veterans.

6. President Lincoln's plan for Reconstruction provided that
   a) Confederate states be kept under martial law for a minimum of ten years, subject to curfews and suspension of the writ of habeas corpus.
   b) at least ten percent of white male residents in a state that had been militarily subdued must take an oath of future loyalty to the Union.
   c) slavery must be gradually ended over a period of thirty years, provided that all children be freed at the age of eighteen.
   d) before a state could resume its own government and send representatives to Congress, it must adopt a constitution abolishing slavery.
   e) any state that had attempted to secede must pay the federal government in specie for the expense that state had cost the federal government by warring on the nation.

7. The Wade-Davis plan passed by Congress and pocket-vetoed by Lincoln required that
   a) half of a seceded state's white male population pledge loyalty to the Union.
   b) each seceded state provide financing through bond sales for a massive program of railroad building across the South.
   c) citizens who could take the Ironclad Oath that they had never supported secession elect delegates to a convention to draw up a state constitution.
   d) at least half the congressional districts in each seceded state have a black majority.
   e) each seceded state grant blacks equality before the law; but the plan had no requirement that equality include the right to vote.

8. During the year of President Andrew Johnson's Reconstruction plan,
   a) estates of any planter owning more than twenty slaves were confiscated and sold.
   b) most rebels received blanket pardons if they pledged loyalty to the Union and support for emancipation.
   c) the Ku Klux Klan was recognized as the president's primary agency for establishing Reconstruction government in former Confederate states.
   d) Johnson attempted to keep enough readmitted states from ratifying the Thirteenth Amendment that it would be defeated.
   e) officials of the defeated Confederate government were elected to Congress, including Alexander Stephens of Georgia, vice president of the Confederacy.

9. Among Black Codes adopted by states President Johnson readmitted to the Union in 1865, typical rules
   a) granted blacks legal rights to marry, hold property, and have some access to the courts.
   b) provided payments to former slaves equivalent to back wages for their last ten years of slave labor.
   c) required black residents to show proof each January of employment for the year.

d) prohibited workers from leaving a plantation without permission from their employer.

e) were consistent in defining blacks alone as the object of their controls.

10. The Reconstruction Plan adopted by Congress in 1867 over President Johnson's veto
   a) disenfranchised all voters in seceded states except for blacks and carpetbaggers.
   b) divided the region from Virginia to Texas into five military districts.
   c) imposed no direct federal rule in Tennessee, already readmitted to the Union.
   d) allocated money for crop price support payments to depressed plantation owners.
   e) required, as conditions for readmitting a former secessionist state, that the state ratify the Fourteenth Amendment and adopt a state constitution giving adult male blacks the vote.

11. Among people in former Confederate states who might support Republican policies were
   a) wealthy industrialists who had opposed the secession effected by their enemies, the cotton planters.
   b) Choctaw, Cherokee, and Seminole.
   c) freed slaves, once their right to vote was firmly established by law.
   d) people in hill and mountain areas who resented domination by wealthy planters.
   e) residents of the lowlands angry at the apparent privileges the Confederacy had given to the rich, or resentful of the misery that secession and war had brought to the South.

12. Delegates to state constitutional conventions in former Confederate states
   a) represented carpetbaggers and freed slaves alone, excluding native white voters.
   b) were elected under laws excluding former Confederate officials, which led many former rebels to refuse to participate in the elections at all.
   c) came in large numbers from the ranks of southern white Unionists and mountaineers.
   d) included carpetbaggers, who made up about one sixth of the total.
   e) united white and black delegates for a program of complete racial equality.

13. Measures popular among southern state constitutional convention delegates included
   a) the first provision for free public education, but in schools separated by race.
   b) plans to prevent freed slaves from voting that were not too obvious.
   c) a general tax on property that increased the levy on landowners.
   d) restricting the power of ex-rebel planters, a policy favored by hill country white Unionists.
   e) immediately replacing all federal troops with local law enforcement.

14. During the period of Klan violence,
   a) the KKK, to give itself an air of respectability, organized charitable relief for widows and orphans of Confederate veterans.
   b) the Klan engaged in whipping, shooting, and hanging known Republican voters, to intimidate both black and white supporters of Reconstruction.
   c) a militia of white Unionists and blacks organized by Arkansas Governor Powell Clayton tried Klan suspects by military commission.
   d) the Klan toured northern states with colorfully costumed vaudeville acts to patch up wartime differences and give a positive view of southern life.
   e) a landowner who had distributed land to his former slaves was whipped, and African Americans who owned or rented their own land were under threat.

15. Political trends and influences that helped bring an end to Reconstruction included
   a) a widespread belief in Congress that the Thirteenth Amendment had been a mistake.
   b) a conviction that the Constitution as amended during Reconstruction provided southern African Americans all the protection they needed.
   c) evangelical revivals that persuaded black voters to abandon political action.
   d) loss of interest by northern voters in the rights of southern African Americans.
   e) a determination on the part of Liberal Republicans to end attacks on "the better sort of people" such as they thought they saw in proposals for inflated currency benefiting labor.

G. ESSAY QUESTIONS OR ORAL REPORTS

1. Write what you think should have been the right plan for Reconstruction of the defeated secessionist states. Define the goals of the plan. Then define what groups in the various former Confederate states might have rallied in support of the plan, and what groups, if any, would have to be crushed or subdued to make it work. Finally, how would your plan have been put into action? What political, economic, and military forces would have to be mobilized?

2. Do some research into how citizens who had remained loyal to the Union within seceded states, or remained apart from the Confederate government, lived in the years after the Civil War. Consider the kinds of people who had been hostile to secession and major geographic areas that resisted Confederate rule. Detail examples of support of emancipation and opposition to it, as well as attitudes toward Black Codes, Reconstruction governments, and Ku Klux Klan activity.

3. Examine how the racial attitudes that took hold after Reconstruction, and gave rise to Jim Crow laws, were cultivated during the 1870s and 1880s to win back white voters who had given support to Republican state governments in the South. This will require some examples of racist rhetoric used, who used it, and in what year, set in chronological order. Where and why did Republican administrations win the support of southern white voters? Who was most motivated to try to break that support?

4. Examine any two leading Liberal Republicans. Look at their politics going back before the Civil War, and see how their thought evolved in response to the war and Reconstruction. Can you say of any of them that they betrayed their earlier principles, or was there some consistency in the development of their thought?

5. Thousands of individuals who made important contributions to Reconstruction are not named in this chapter: teachers, entrepreneurs, governors, sheriffs, congressmen, soldiers, farmers, to mention a few. Look up some of them, select one or more, and prepare a biographical or historical summary of the life and accomplishments of whoever you have chosen. Relate the experiences that brought your choice or choices to the events of Reconstruction. What changes may the Civil War and Reconstruction have made in the views and motivations of your one or more individuals?

Printed and bound by CPI Group (UK) Ltd, Croydon, CR0 4YY

13/04/2025

14656568-0005